HOW SURFING RUINED MY LIFE

How Surfing Ruined My Life: 30 Years of Riding Waves and One Year Trying Not To is published under Catharsis, a sectionalized division under Di Angelo Publications, Inc.

Catharsis is an imprint of Di Angelo Publications.

Printed in the United States of America.

Di Angelo Publications

Library of Congress
How Surfing Ruined My Life: 30 Years of Riding Waves
and One Year Trying Not To
ISBN: 978-1-962603-47-8
Paperback

Words: Jason Borte
Cover Design: Savina Deianova
Interior Design: Kimberly James
Editors: Matt Samet, Willy Rowberry

Downloadable via www.dapbooks.shop
and other e-book retailers.

For educational, business, and bulk orders, contact distribution@diangelopublications.com.

1. Biography & Autobiography --- Adventurers & Explorers
2. Sports & Recreation --- Water Sports --- Surfing
3. Body, Mind, & Spirit --- Healing --- General

HOW SURFING RUINED MY LIFE

30 Years of Riding Waves and One Year Trying Not To

JASON BORTE

To my brother for leading, my parents for trusting,
my friends for pushing, my kids for inspiring,
and my wife for everything.

CONTENTS

NOVEMBER 2013

I look over my shoulder toward land. Ravaged, overbuilt, confining, stagnant, dry, miserable land. We've done our worst to it, reshaping every inch to allow more and more people to squeeze aboard. Is that really where I want to spend the next year of my life? Can I possibly survive that?

Seconds earlier, I rode a wave, roughly the one-hundred-thousandth of the last thirty-some years, carving my signature into a chunky, liquid skate ramp, almost literally walking on water, knowing full well that at that same instant, much of humanity was staring at a screen, or sitting in some form of traffic, or daydreaming of doing something else with their lives, literally anything. And an epiphany formulated in my subconscious, an idea that, if acted upon, would make me...just...like...them.

Solo surf sessions provide an opportunity to leave the world behind. At 43, I haven't been forcing myself to paddle out alone enough. Surfing with friends or with my son brings instant gratification regardless of the conditions. These days, if I have no one to surf with, I often won't surf at all. But there, bobbing in the ocean at the North End of Virginia Beach with no one around, I'm reminded how surfing by oneself leads to an inevitable journey into the subconscious. And sometimes, as I've just learned, what I find there freaks me out. Sometimes, I stumble onto an idea that shouldn't be stumbled upon.

I try to shake off this epiphany as soon as I become aware of it, but it refuses to be ignored. As it marinates inside my brain, the possible ramifications of such a move stack upon one another like a barrage of Tetris blocks until they obscure my field of vision.

Now that I contemplate going through with it, chills run up my spine. Not the I'm-freezing-my-nuts-off chills, although it's a gray, 50-degree late-November day and I'm bobbing in windblown, equally cold water. Those chills will come later, buffeted by northeast gusts as I strip out of my wetsuit. No, I'm talking about the other kind of chills, the sort that come from blasting "Purple Rain" on the car radio, or melting into the eyes of your newborn baby, or sensing a hungry shark zeroing in on you with open jaws. The chills that come from overwhelming beauty, or love, or fear, from the contemplation of stepping out of life as you know it.

As the magnitude of what I'm considering settles in, I feel the eyes of the world on me. I gasp, and whip my head from one end of the beach to the other to see if anyone is around. Fortunately, there's not another human in sight—aside from a bunch of seagulls, the beach is devoid of life. Thank goodness. The word hasn't yet spread.

Still, the idea doesn't feel safe. I need to contain it, afraid of what might happen were it to escape. If I tell anyone, if someone else finds out about it, I'll feel obligated to do it. The notion bounces off the walls of my skull, taunting me with dares of 'You won't do it; you're too scared.'

I can still quash the blasphemous thought, never speak of it, and no one will know I birthed such a ridiculous concept, much less entertained it.

So, I let it go, catch-and-release style, freeing it into the Atlantic to live out its life safely under the sea, or, if it wants, to ride the current down the coast and latch onto some other unsuspecting surfer.

My attention turns to getting a few more rides as the daylight wanes. *'Not thinking about anything. La-dee-dah. Just looking around for a wave to catch.'*

I wait, and a welcome distraction comes in the sudden urge to empty my bladder. And as any (honest) surfer will tell you, peeing while surfing in cold water isn't a bad thing. Even with today's wetsuit technology, warmth remains a coveted resource. Plus, eliminating all bodily waste will help me to mentally release the epiphany that now threatens my way of life.

'Ahhh.' I let it flow, and I instantly feel warmer and better.

But this idea doesn't want to be freed. It swims hard against the current and sneaks its way inside my suit, boring into my body as if it were the candiru, the Amazonian "penis fish" that allegedly swims up your urethra when you pee, then deploys thousands of tiny spikes to lodge itself inside its new host.

"Oh, I'm staying," the idea insists, "right...fucking... here."

I don't so much decide to go through with it as get swamped by it. The idea wasn't there, and now it is. And I'm so intrigued by the social-experiment side of it that I have no choice but to succumb.

It's settled. I'm quitting surfing.

I recently read an article on the idea of stopping surfing, and the author, after loads of research and interviews, reached the conclusion that it doesn't happen. Surfers fade away due to injuries or work or family obligations, but no avid waterman voluntarily returns to landlubbing. Quitting isn't an option. Surfing is too much fun, too desirable a way of life to abandon. As any enthusiast will attest, a bad day in the ocean shits all over a good day of practically anything else.

Still, there I am, staring into the abyss of this other life, one I left long ago. An existence where people stop what they're doing and run indoors whenever rain begins to fall, where people fear what lurks beneath the water, where an approaching hurricane is reason to stay away from the beach, and where having solid ground beneath one's feet is viewed as a good thing.

Over 99 percent of humans live full lives without ever riding a single wave, but that doesn't mean it's okay. I'm among a relatively small tribe, roughly the size of the cult of Scientology, and no less wacky to noninitiates.

Worldwide estimates in the neighborhood of five million are tough to substantiate, and the number of dedicated wave slaves likely falls short of seven figures. My religion of choice is, in many ways, a healthy one, but one that nevertheless requires such devotion that it engulfs every other aspect of my life. And I'm about to throw it away.

Not forever, I tell myself, but for one full year. That's a serious chunk of time, a more-than-worthy challenge. For thirty years, I've only gone multiple weeks without surfing on two occasions, and those were due to cracked ribs and a high ankle sprain. But fifty-two straight weeks, by choice?

Challenges fascinate me. I went one month drinking nothing but water, just because of an argument with friends about who would give up first. Another time, after a few beers, I got up and ran 10 miles when a friend bet me I couldn't. I'd never run in my life, but it was nothing more than putting one foot in front of the other, over and over again. This was another story. For the average person, abstaining from riding a wave for 365 days would be just another year. For me, turning my back on the sea will be the most difficult thing I've done in my life. And I'm not even sure what would be second.

I have a master's degree, am a pro surfing champion, have owned a surf school since 1997, have written two books about surfing, teach eighth grade in a public school, and have a stable, twenty-year marriage that's produced three wonderful children. I've done plenty. It's just that none of it seems too difficult, nothing on the level of losing my religion, cold turkey.

Moments later, I'm back at our home a block from the beach and into dry clothes, resolute and ready to drop the news on my family. The' only known me as a rabid surfer, so their lives stand to change dramatically. I'm about to have a boatload of free time, so, like it or not, my wife and kids are going to be seeing a lot more of me. Chasing waves has caused me to miss more than my share of birthdays, anniversaries, teacher conferences, ball games, and ballet recitals. Still, my love for them isn't in question. If asked, they'll say they're the most important thing in my life, right up there with riding waves. (In truth, they're way more important to me than surfing, but, from their perspective, it would be close.)

I start by telling Mrs. Borte. We've been together since high school, all told twenty-five years. She never surfed, but she's been around the beach forever, even before she knew me. She acknowledges surfing's position as the true love of my life, and deals with it grudgingly. When I tell her I'm quitting, her predictable response is, "Yeah, right. You're not serious." She won't believe it until she sees it.

Then, I tell my oldest son, Grady, the only other surfer in the family. A high-schooler with little to no interest in academics, he's only recently become more surfer than skater, and more often than not is in the water with friends. Grady understands the allure of a challenge, so he asks, "Why not surf every day for a year, instead?" Too easy—plenty of people have done that.

My middle-schooler daughter's reaction is priceless. The only time Mia has been on a board was years earlier, when she was put on restriction and told she could earn her privileges back by riding three waves. She stood up on her first try, quickly got two more, rode the last one straight to the beach, stepped off on dry sand, and never looked back. Despite her distaste for surfing, Mia is more like me than any of my children. In many ways, we seem to share the same brain. We can look at each other and immediately know what the other is thinking. "Whaaaaaat!" she screams when I say I'm quitting. "It's like you're not even my dad anymore. You're just some random, old guy that tells me what to do."

My youngest son, Hudson, stands to benefit more than anyone. Most of my free time will be spent taking him and his cousins and friends on fun adventures around town. At five, he's too young to understand what's going on or to have an opinion on it.

Finally, I call Smitty, my oldest surfing friend and favorite person to share a session with. Smitty works for the city of Virginia Beach as a highway inspector, and he's sort of the unofficial mayor of our local spot, 1st Street. Everybody knows Smitty. My favorite thing about him is his storytelling. I've heard them all—the pranks, the fights, the ridiculous situations he finds himself in on a daily basis—but I never get tired of hearing them again. He told me about the article on quitting, and he's about to lose his trusty surfing companion. "That's cool," Smitty replies, and I think he means it. After all, without me in the water next to him, he'll be free to catch a lot more waves.

The coming 365 days rise in front of me like an endless procession of towering swells I'll have to paddle through. I'm bracing to take each one on the head. And when I finally emerge out the back, I have no idea what will be waiting for me.

As much as I expect to be miserable, I anticipate the opportunity to creep out of my surfing cocoon and discover what's out there. I'll soon be questioning every aspect of my existence. Each moment will present a challenge, and when it's over, my life will be forever changed.

1981

Waves, as far as I know, are for karate chopping. When he was growing up, my dad's favorite pastime, aside from playing pool, was street fighting, so he sends us to Chuck Norris Karate Studios to follow in his footsteps. Chuck drops by the studio on occasion, to collect some money and sign a few autographs. The endless list of hyperbolic Chuck 'facts' isn't yet invented, but he's already a star, having headlined several action movies including my fave, *Good Guys Wear Black*. Inside the dojo, my older brother, Derrick, rises to red belt, which is just below black. I'm mired in green, unable to perform my moves with enough panache to graduate to the next level. Meanwhile, the ocean, on our rare visits, provides the perfect medium for practicing our moves. We stand in the shorebreak, punching, kicking, and chopping approaching waves as if they're a gang of minions sent to kill us.

In 1975, we moved from Norfolk, where I was born, to a newly built suburb in Virginia Beach called Green Run. We're only 10 miles from the oceanfront, but it may as well be 1,000. The beach, to us, is a low-budget theme park that we see maybe once each year and otherwise don't think about.

Spending one's childhood sitting in the house, staring at a screen, fortunately doesn't exist. Cable television hasn't yet exploded, and home video games are limited to the handheld Mattel Football or Atari Pong. Either way, there's nothing more than a few dots or lines or a black screen, hardly capable of captivating one's attention. We also have electronic football, the metal field populated by tiny plastic players vibrating through simulated plays. We spend hours prepping our teams with paint and stick-on numbers, but my players never go where I want them to. Instead, they buzz around in circles as if blindfolded.

I have a BMX bike and free reign of the neighborhood, so I'm on the move from morning till the streetlights come on. Aside from karate, my childhood is all about baseball, BMX, and lots of football. I'm perennially among the smallest in my class, and I'm not a standout on the football field, yet I somehow convince myself that professional football is my future.

My neighborhood tackle team of 95-pounders has a scrimmage game against Derrick's team of 110-pounders. On one play, I'm lined up on defense, right across from my brother. Derrick is bigger, faster, and stronger, and he knows it. He calls over to his quarterback to indicate, "Hey, look who's trying to cover me." The ball is snapped, and Derrick makes an aggressive step upfield, sending me backwards to stay ahead of him. Derrick freezes, and the quarterback zips a screen pass to him. I gather my wits and zero in for the tackle. I dive, and Derrick sidesteps, leaving me face-down in the dirt. I look back in time to see my brother high-stepping into the end zone. I should realize that I'm not destined for football greatness, but I'm not ready to give up.

When there aren't enough neighborhood players around for a pickup game, we only need a few kids for "Smear the Queer." The game has nothing to do with sexual orientation; later, as political correctness takes root, it's apparently renamed "Kill the man with the ball." (This doesn't have quite the same ring to it, but the new name does offer a more appropriate description.) One kid, "The Queer," has the football, and he runs around until he gets tackled. Since there's no end zone, you run in circles like aimless little electronic football players. When you get tackled, you toss the ball into the air and another "Queer" snatches it and runs. I'm small, and not very fast, but I rule at Smear the Queer. Flat-out speed isn't necessary, since there's no finish line or goal posts. The key is an ability to make instant adjustments to avoid being tackled, and I have that skill in abundance.

Green Run is a new development of tract homes, a lower-middle-class neighborhood with kids of every color. For my elementary-school years, my best friends are two Black kids, Chucky and Brehon, both of whom share similar interests. As far as I'm concerned, we're all just kids. Sure, all of their furniture is covered with clear plastic, but when we skin our knees in the street, all our blood comes out looking the same shade of red.

Chucky's mom is a schoolteacher, and she insists on him and his siblings speaking proper English. His favorite snack is sugar packets, and his special talent is being able to vomit on command. I convince him to demonstrate his skill for each new kid on our street. "Hey, Chucky," I say, "this kid doesn't believe you can throw up." Chucky grins, preparing to prove his mettle. He squats to steady himself, spreads his hands like a magician for dramatic effect, and then starts gulping down air like he's just emerged from under water. Within seconds, he gurgles a few times, and voila—puke.

Brehon can't barf on call, but he's one cool brotha'. I watch *Good Times* on TV, and then I see the same lively and loving family dynamic at Brehon's house around the corner. Usually, though, whenever we go inside to refuel, it's at my house. There's less yelling there, and our pantry never seems to run low on snacks. Brehon and I run the 'skreet' and share dreams of making it to the NFL. (Brehon's older brother Wesley, who is good friends with Derrick, will eventually find his way onto an NFL roster.)

If Smear the Queer becomes a professional sport, I may have a future. My goal is to be a running back, and in the field behind my house, I almost never get tackled. As it stands, my football career peaks with a single in-game kickoff return during a game in my neighborhood league. I catch the ball and take off upfield. One defender falls in front of me, so I'm faced with a snap decision. I should use him as a shield, have his teammates slow up and give me an opportunity to dart around them, but I don't. Instead, I leap over him. Derrick is impressed, which is rare—that's enough for me. I land, and the rest of the defense is waiting for me. From every direction, they pile on. My training has prepared me to handle the weight of a few kids on my back, but not this many. There's no escape.

We've lost our last couple games, and I think our quarterback, a kid named Peanut, is the problem. At practice, when the coaches aren't close by, I call Peanut out in front of the team. He goes crying to the coach, and there goes my shot at ever getting another kick return, much less playing running back. With that, my NFL dreams fall flat into the dirt.

In baseball, I find slightly more success. My team is atrocious, but I'm among the better players. My coaches are two 18-year-old studs, and they put my smartass nature to good use. In one game, the ump makes some terrible calls, and to get back at him, my coaches instruct me to do whatever I can to piss him off during my next turn at bat.

Before the pitcher can get off a single pitch, I call "time" and ask the ump to clean off the plate. He does, and I step back into the box. Then, as the pitcher prepares to throw, I call "time" again, stepping out to knock the dirt off my cleats. Next time, I stop the show to tuck my jersey in. I look to my coaches, and they're rolling around the dugout with laughter. After that, I pause to pull up my socks. When I ask the ump again to clean the plate, he's had enough. He goes to my coaches, who barely hold it together, and tells them he's about to throw me out of the game. The act has gone on long enough, and they instruct me to go ahead and hit. By this time, the pitcher is too rattled to throw a strike, so I get to first base on a walk.

My specialty on the baseball diamond is getting out of pickles. A pickle is when a runner is stranded between two bases, and the fielders on either side of him toss the ball back and forth until one of them gets close enough to tag him out. Whenever I get on base, I take a huge lead off base, hoping to get into a pickle. It's sort of like Smear the Queer, but in baseball. I run back and forth between the bases until one of the fielders, inevitably, makes a bad throw. Then, I'm home free, darting to the next base and beyond, looking to engage them in another pickle.

I play a bunch of different positions, and I eventually get a shot at pitching. Nolan Ryan, the king of strikeouts, is my hero. On Sundays, I scan the sports section to see his stats. My parents buy me one of those cheap pitching nets that, if the ball hits it squarely, bounces it back to you. I spend hours honing my fastball, dodging backyard dog-poop mines the whole time. For my age, the teams play three innings of T-ball and three of pitch. I beg my coaches to give me a shot, and, at last, I'm scheduled to throw during the pitch innings.

My first pitch misses the mark. Ball one. Same with the next, and two more after that. I walk my first batter. The next one is no different. Four pitches, four balls. It's my first outing, and I'm already in trouble. Two runners on base, and no outs. Hell, I haven't even thrown a strike. My coaches halt the game and run out to the mound for a pep talk. "You okay?" they ask.

"Yeah, I'm good," I lie. They tell me to settle down and throw strikes, but I know what they're really saying is, "If you don't start throwing strikes, you're gone." My margin for error is gone. I focus. My next pitch goes for a strike, as do the following two. "Strike three, yerrout," screams the umpire to the batter. My first strikeout! I do the same thing for all but one of the batters over three innings. Eight strikeouts in all, and my team wins. I'm destined to be the next Nolan Ryan.

Derrick plays in the league above mine, and his shot as a pitcher goes somewhat differently. I started a bit off target, but his pitching is nothing short of wild. Tarzan-level wild. He whizzes a couple fastballs for strikes, but the other balls miss by a wide margin. One, somehow, is not just outside the strike zone but completely over the backstop, which is a good twenty feet high. His coaches yank him out before he can hurt someone. For that instant, I've bested Derrick at something. After a decade in his shadow, I'm finally out. Take that, big brother!

The following week, I'm back on the pitcher's mound. The scouts haven't descended on our Green Run Little League complex yet, but another few games like the last one, and word will spread. I start my second game just like the first one, walking two consecutive batters. My coaches trot out, only this time, they don't give me a pep talk or another chance. I'm banished from the mound, never to return. I can't even outdo my brother, much less Nolan Ryan.

Derrick isn't horrible as far as older siblings go. When

none of his friends are around, he lets me hang out with him. When we get into fights, I make him laugh so hard that he's defenseless. I never endure the sort of physical abuse some kids get from their big brothers, and we get along well. On the other hand, he's wicked smart, as in Mensa level, and he uses his intelligence to stay way ahead of his little brother. He calls the shots, and I remain firmly in his wake.

My childhood is pretty close to idyllic. As the middle child (my sister, Nikki, comes along four years after me), I never get into trouble. If anything happens, it's got to be Derrick's fault—and more often than not, it *is* Derrick's fault. He's kind of an "evil" genius, setting examples for me such as toasting frogs with a magnifying glass, locking people in port-a-potties, and pushing around kids who are smaller than him. Still, we have a loving home life, heaps of snacks in the pantry, and the freedom to explore our surroundings. That doesn't mean I don't have problems.

For one thing, I have a slight urination issue. Okay, I'm a massive bed wetter. I'm not sure if I can't physically wake up in the night to pee, or if I'm too lazy. Either way, I'm glad we have a tall fence in the backyard, since my mom regularly puts my piss-stained mattress out back to dry in the sun. As a last resort, my parents purchase the Wee Alert, a square plastic sheet attached to a buzzer that delivers a tiny shock at the first sign of wetness. I pee, and it buzzes me awake. After a few weeks of waking up to this electric-shock therapy, I'm cured.

The other "problem" is that I'm also pretty smart. Not Derrick-level smart, but who is? At school, probably based solely on the fact that I'm his little brother, I'm tested for our school district's gifted program, and I pass. One day a week, I carpool to a special school to be with other like-minded students. Derrick has moved to junior high, and the only other student who attends the gifted program from my school happens to be the dirtiest kid on Earth. He lives right down the street in a house that, if the health department ever bothered to step foot into, would be condemned. His animals pee and poop on the floor, and nobody bothers to clean it up. Thinking about the stench still triggers my gag reflex.

So, I have to carpool to school every other week with Dirt Boy in his family's station wagon. The thirty-minute-trip in their dumpster-on-wheels leaves me gasping for air. I don't want to put the burden on my mom to drive me every week, so I keep the ordeal to myself. Eventually, the trauma becomes too much, and I come up with some excuse to drop out of the program in the fifth grade.

Judging from my teachers' comments throughout my early school years, I'm not such a joy to have in class. "Jason needs to learn that there is a time and place for his 'humor,'" writes one teacher on my report card. "He must improve his conduct. His mouth is causing him problems!"

On the other hand, I no longer sleep in a puddle of my own urine, and I don't need to hold my breath on the way to school. Life is as good as it gets. Then, out of the blue, my parents say we're moving. They own a couple convenience stores inside bank buildings downtown, and business is booming so much that they decide, like George Jefferson, that we're movin' on up to the East Side. A nicer neighborhood and a bigger house don't matter to me. I expected life in the hood with Chucky and Brehon to go on forever, so the news is a sucker punch. Wherever we're going, I just hope they have Smear the Queer.

DECEMBER 2013

Few people have heard of a guy from Bologna named Ugo Boncompagni, but he plays a major role in the timing of my surfing sabbatical. In his 30s, Ugo was a schoolteacher. (Sound familiar?) Later in his life—on May 13, 1572, to be exact—because some dudes in robes blew white smoke out of the Sistine Chapel chimney, Ugo became Pope Gregory XIII and took over a thing called "The Catholic Church." He reformed stuff and started some colleges, but he's most notable for commissioning the Gregorian calendar, the one everybody uses today.

So, since I'm undertaking this journey to live like the common man, I decide to begin my year off surfing on January 1. Calendars, all neatly divided into easily digested months, come in handy for missions such as this. The 2014 new year is only a few weeks away, and it'll be one less date I need to remember. Besides, I've already booked a trip to Puerto Rico for my family for the end of December, and there isn't a chance in hell I'll spend money on an island trip and not go surfing.

Money and I have always had a weird relationship. I've never craved it or cared enough about it to learn how to make it work for me. I tend to spend whatever I have, and then figure out how to get some more, which is fine, I suppose, if you're single and have no dependents. However, as a husband and parent, that's a recipe for disaster.

Over the previous dozen years, Mrs. B and I spent a bunch of money that we didn't have. In 2000, we built a house we could barely afford. Fortunately, the house was in a nice neighborhood near the beach, so the value constantly increased. Within a couple years, we racked up some debt and remedied that by refinancing to take out the equity. A couple years after that, we did it again, this time borrowing even more dough to build a needless addition on the house. After that, we recklessly burned through a line of credit, and by 2012, we were riddled with debt and unable to stop the bleeding.

We didn't want to sell the house, so we rented it out and packed our entire family—two parents, three kids, and two dogs—into a tiny two-bedroom apartment beneath my parents' house. In effect, I moved into my parents' basement. The kids were understandably bummed, but we sold them on the idea of being able to take more trips with all the money we'd be saving.

Which brings us to Puerto Rico, which for East Coasters is sort of a poor man's Hawaii. Puerto Rico is easy to get to, relatively cheap, and since it's a US territory, there's no hassling with passports and immigration lines. And there's tons of surf. As Donald Trump described it in 2017 when visiting to toss out paper-towel rolls after Hurricane Maria, "This is an island, surrounded by water. Big water."

I've been to Puerto Rico a handful of times for competitions or just surf getaways, but for the rest of my squad this will be their first visit. Nearly every trip We've taken, first as a couple and later as a family, has revolved around surfing. And this one will be no different. We even bring my brother-in-law Keegan, another avid surfer, along. Thus, the field is evened with three in search of waves and three getting dragged around to whichever beach we deem to be the best spot to surf. No one complains, though, seeing as how We've fled the midwinter blues for a tropical island.

I sprinkle in just enough touristy excursions—a waterfall, a giant cave with a beautiful window view—to avoid a mutiny. Still, near the end of the week, Mrs. B rightfully demands an afternoon of sea-glass gathering. She does her homework and locates the optimal spot, and I corral everyone into our minivan. Thirty minutes later, we arrive at the spot, or as close as we can drive to it. The actual spot is a lengthy hike down the beach.

Mrs. B steps out, and no one else budges. "Fine, I'll go by myself," she harrumphs, and tromps away. The rest of us head for the surfing beach and return a few hours later to pick her up. It's my last week of surfing before the sabbatical, so I have to maximize my time in the water.

The next morning, the last of the trip, I drag the whole brood to a spot called Middles, an out-of-the-way beach that boasts some of the best surf on the island. But not today. There's a solid swell, a little overhead and packing a hefty punch. Yet the wind is all wrong, howling onshore and chopping what should be lengthy, tapered lines into short, pancaking sections. On the positive side, the subpar conditions keep the crowds to a minimum.

Keegan and Grady hop in the water, and I take to gathering driftwood and fallen palm fronds to construct a makeshift shelter from the beating sun. By the time I finish and make my way into the surf, the boys are over it. They've each taken their share of beatings and want to find a spot that's better suited for the winds. The other surfers likely have the same idea, so everyone has vacated the lineup.

While no one else seems to care for the conditions, I'm in my element. Soft waves bore me after a while, so to re-create the feeling that hooked me on surfing so long ago, I need a wave with a little punch. And that's what Middles delivers. I get a few fun rides and sit alone in the lineup. Robbed of the opportunity for idle banter, my mind turns inward. And we know what that can lead to. The weight of my impending decision descends on me. The next day will be December 31st, and we'll be traveling home. After that, it'll be January 1st. So, this is it, my final session.

I'm bidding farewell to the most enduring relationship of my life. The situation is purely coincidental, but it's as if one of the surfers whispered to the others, "Hey, let's leave the two of them alone." As far as goodbyes go, the setting can't be much better. What I feel sitting alone in the lineup isn't sadness; it's excitement. I'm taking on a massive challenge, one that will test me on a daily basis.

I'll get to find out what I'm made of.

Paulo Coelho wrote in *The Alchemist*, "When someone makes a decision, he is really diving into a strong current that will carry him to places he had never dreamed of." What will those places look like for me? I have no clue, but I am about to find out.

And there will be plenty of time to find out, but for now, a meaty wave approaches and smacks me back into the moment. Despite its surface-level imperfections, this wave is the most beautiful thing I've ever seen. While I'm usually not one to mythologize the act of surfing, under the circumstances, this wave is as meaningful as any I've encountered. I swing around and paddle a few strokes, and the energy contained in this single swell lifts me over the moon. In that instant, I am 12 again, every cell of my body attuned to the rhythm of the ocean. To a surfer, navigating a wave of consequence must come close to a Buddhist experiencing enlightenment. I don't ride the wave so much as immerse myself in its spirit.

Regardless of how much importance I assign to this ride, the wave's going to do what the wave's going to do. Thanks to the swell, the tide, and the wind, Mother Nature has decreed that this one won't offer up any sort of epic tube ride, or even an opportunity to run my hand along the lip and enjoy a few seconds of blissful glide. The cascading crest is violent and forceful, the reef menacing beneath me. My nirvana moment will be but a blip, and blowing it carries serious repercussions.

Thankfully, a century of advancements in materials

technology and surfboard design has brought equipment a long way since the days of Duke or Gidget. My trusty steed is about my height, 5'7", and it's far sleeker than my dad bod. I get to my feet as the lip pitches, and I beat it to the trough in time to redirect back up the face. Just before detonation, I twist toward the beach and whip the board beneath me. The explosion of water meeting coral is something out of an action movie, and I skirt beyond its reach on my way to my family. They're waiting impatiently to go do something, anything, else.

Grady and Keegan, unable to adapt to the challenging conditions like they'd hoped, didn't have much fun at Middles. A couple hours before dark, they want me to drive to check out a spot called Wilderness. I'm content, satisfied I've ridden enough waves for not only that day and that trip, but possibly for my entire life. I've had my moment, that perfect communion-with-nature experience. In my head, I've already begun my self-imposed exile. They want redemption. We pack the minivan and head toward Wilderness.

Due to the beach's orientation at Wilderness, the surf is much cleaner. Wilderness is also smaller and more user-friendly, which always translates to more crowded. It would be a shame to paddle into a pack and potentially ruin my earlier moment. I can kick back on the sand and enjoy the peacefulness, removed from the fray. I try, but I can't escape the nagging fact that I'm hours from heading home to the cold to burrow my way through a 365-day-thick pile of shit. Despite the crowd, the water is clear and inviting, and the sun feels so warm against my skin. I have no choice but to paddle out for yet another last hurrah.

Bad idea.

Crowded lineups lead to frustration even at home, where, as a longtime local, I'm typically afforded enough space to snag a few waves no matter how packed it is. On a faraway island, especially one where machismo runs rampant, there's nothing worse than squabbling over a limited supply of waves like a flock of seagulls fighting over French fries. As soon as I hit the lineup, I see it's a mistake.

In forty minutes of waiting and paddling, I catch two piddly waves and get snaked by other surfers both times. In a few other instances, I paddle but have to give way to people in better position. Finally, after an over-expenditure of effort with no discernible reward, a decent-sized bump heads right toward me. A couple other guys are paddling on the shoulder, but this one is all mine. I head down the line and eye a small section of steep-enough wave face that will permit me to lay into a turn, to release the frustration the session has caused. Before I reach the spot, however, a miniature projectile—just large enough to impede any progress— catapults directly in front of me. It's a tiny human, eight or nine years old, squatting with a wide, stink-butt stance, atop an equally small surfboard. At the last second, the boy's dad has launched him onto the wave in front of me. I can't be mad at the kid; he's simply holding on for the ride.

Back in the lineup, someone who clearly knows the dad says, "Don't push your kid in front of people." The dad, a burly dude whose forced Spanglish accent exposes him as a transplanted wannabe local, replies, "Aww, they've had enough waves in their lives."

The blood inside my head turns to steam, but then I realize the idiot dad, likely a construction worker based on the size of his biceps, has hit the nail on the head. I should be content with my magical earlier session. There's no reason for me to be back out here. I have absolutely ridden enough waves, waves of all shapes and sizes, and in faraway places that most people will never get to see. I've ridden enough waves not just for one person, but for several lifetimes.

It is said that the fool learns nothing from the wise man, but that the wise man learns much from the fool. I silently thank the asshole dad and catch the next whitewater to the beach, wondering all along which of us was the fool in this parable: the one still in the water having fun with his son, or the one bellyboarding toward the beach for a self-imposed year in drydock?

1982

We load up our frumpy station wagon, soon to be dumped in favor of a Mercedes sedan more appropriate to our new neighborhood, and head across town. My only consolation to leaving my entire life behind in Green Run is that, since we are headed to a new area, Derrick doesn't have friends either. He'll have no choice but to hang out with his little brother, or so I think.

We are still nowhere near the beach, but to our more affluent neighbors, the beach isn't so much a destination as a way of life. *Fast Times at Ridgemont High* arrives this summer, opening my eyes to the beach lifestyle. Derrick is in ninth grade, and his outgoing nature makes it easy for him to attract a new group of friends. This crew isn't content with cruising around the neighborhood. They venture all the way to the Virginia Beach Oceanfront, five miles away, and they do so without parents. For some unknown reason, someone gives my dad a couple of old longboards. The yellowed logs do nothing but lean against our fence and get yellower due in equal parts to the sun and our urinating dogs.

Seemingly overnight, Derrick loses interest in everything We've done to this point. He ditches organized sports, trades his BMX bike for a beach cruiser, and announces he's getting his own surfboard. The mammoth boards in our backyard won't cut it; he must have a fresh shortboard. I watch in awe as he sketches up a color design, and a few weeks later my dad drives him to some "surfboard factory" to pick up his new vehicle. It's not enough that I'm forced to abandon my friends; now I also must say goodbye to baseballs and footballs. I technically could still pursue those dreams, but Derrick is the arbiter of what is cool, and he decides surfing is it. Sadly, I come to grips with the fact that I'll never walk the grass in an NFL stadium.

Derrick comes home one day with an issue of *Surfing* magazine, and, page by glorious page, I immerse myself in this foreign world of swashbuckling adventure, as well as something else that catches my eye: bikini-clad boobs. The sport has changed dramatically since the days of *Gidget* and Malibu, when everyone rode 9–10' longboards, basically the station wagons of the surfing world. In the 1970s, waves like Hawaii's Banzai Pipeline came into vogue, causing equipment to trend narrow and pointy to let surfers navigate the massive tubes—a design that's awful, however, when you're trying to fit into the sloped dribblers of Virginia Beach.

By the early '80s, surfers are looking to "get rad" like their skateboarding brethren, and boards become relatively short and fat, which prove ideal for gutless East Coast waves. Furthermore, the long hair and monochromatic, single-finned boards of the '70s are replaced by a new wave of spiked dos and colorful, multi-finned boards. Surfers no longer rock bell-bottoms or flow with waves; instead, they attack them with punk-rock bravado. And surf competition, which was "uncool" for much of the previous decade, enjoys a resurgence, from a bustling world tour on down to a local amateur scene that makes Little League seem stodgy.

Whatever era I stumble upon—'60s logs, '70s guns, '80s rip sticks, or even modern Costco foamies—is irrelevant. If Derrick is into surfing, I dive in headfirst. My magazine studies help me unwrap my mind from the idea that waves are for karate chopping. I've done a bit of skateboarding back in Green Run, and it now dawns on me that the ocean is one massive, moving skatepark. After seeing it all laid out in full color, I'm determined to get to the beach to find out for myself. And since Derrick isn't about to let me tag along with his new crew, I have to find another way.

Salvation arrives one unassuming Saturday afternoon in the form of my favorite aunt, Kathy, who comes to babysit me and my sister while my parents are out. She's the only babysitter I've known, often hanging with us while my parents go for a weekend dinner at a real restaurant and return home with exotic paper drink umbrellas. Kathy has a new man in her life, a wildish dude named Billy who, rumor has it, is a surfer himself.

That afternoon, Kathy says she'll show me "the place where everyone surfs," which, in Virginia Beach, can only mean 1st Street Jetty. As we drive toward the beach,

I can't wait to see my *Surfing* magazine visions come to life—all previous visits to the beach are wiped from memory. This is now the surfing beach; I'm envisioning the heroic waves I pore over in the mag every time I use the bathroom. There's a slight problem: Those waves travel across other oceans, arrive in other countries, break along other coastlines. No one bothers to tell me that Virginia Beach, and much of the East Coast for that matter, is a shitty place to surf.

Actual surfing destinations—places where people travel with the express intention of surfing—have legitimate waves. On the East Coast, we're happy if we get one decent swell per month, a day that a consensus of surfers from around the world would look at and say, "That looks fun." The rest of the time, people still surf, but it's in tiny spurts before hitting the sand.

So, as we make our way to the beach at 1st Street, I'm befuddled by what I see, or what I don't see. The surf appears much the same as during my other visits: small, brownish and crumbly. It's as if the magazines lied to me. What I soon realize is that you have to dig deep to find pictures from the East Coast. *Surfing* magazine operates on its own version of Jim Crow laws, relegating our meager waves and unsightly water to the back pages. And who can blame them? Nobody wants to see that stuff. Sure, when the swell of the year hits Cape Hatteras during hurricane season, the pics warrant a few glossy pages, but otherwise it's the back of the bus for us.

Despite the dreadful surf conditions, 1st Street delivers on its promise of being "the place where everyone surfs." In fact, we happen to arrive during a competition run by the Eastern Surfing Association (ESA), an amateur organization that boasts chapters up and down the coast. There are some trucks on the beach, a few tents, a small PA system, and a few dozen people enjoying the afternoon. Such a miniscule percentage of surfing centers on contests, as evidenced by the rinky-dink setup in front of us. I don't think it can be overstated that the first time I see someone ride a wave, it's in competition.

Although I've experienced my share of competitive sports—from football, to baseball, to karate, to BMX—something fascinates me about what's going on here. The competitors aren't chasing a ball atop some manicured field under the watchful eye of referees blowing whistles. Instead, the surfers paddle, unaccompanied, straight out to sea, which in my world may as well be the edge of the earth.

Aunt Kathy's boyfriend is eager to be accepted into the family, and upon hearing about my interest in surfing, Wild Billy produces a board that's been gathering dust in his garage. He wants it back at some point (presumably so it can sit there again for several years before being tossed out, which is what eventually happens), but I'm free to ride the loaner for as long as I want.

The specifics of the board are irrelevant to me, so long as I'm on my way to join Derrick in the ocean. As it turns out, the borrowed board is a good fit, an all-yellow, 5'7" Hansen twin-fin made in California. It's thick, meaning it offers ample flotation for my 85-pound frame, while its short length provides some maneuverability.

Nowadays, kids learn to surf on much longer soft-boards, often in a surf school under the tutelage of a host of instructors. The instructors ferry the students into the lineup, place them in position, push them into a wave, and yell at them when it's time to stand up. Literally, the only thing required of a modern grom is to pop up from his stomach to his feet. And if he can't do that, not to worry; the instructors simply prop him atop the board before the wave arrives, then shove him into the thing already standing. Thankfully, surf schools don't exist in 1982, at least along the East Coast. If I want to ride a wave, I'll have to hunt one down on my own.

At my new elementary school, I come into a connection to surfing in a roundabout way. When we first move, Derrick and I are still into BMX, and we sometimes pedal up to the local bike shop to hang out. At the shop, I see a kid from my class come in with his mom to pick out a bike. The one he chooses, according to the laughing salesperson, is meant for toddlers. The salesman directs them toward a more appropriate bike, and the kid reluctantly agrees. I chuckle but remain out of sight. When, sometime later, the school-cafeteria chat turns to BMX, this same kid brags of his cool, new bike. I haven't yet made any friends, so here's my chance to shine. I chime in with news of the "baby bike," and everyone gets a good laugh at this kid's expense. I've humiliated him in front of his friends, but at least I'm accepted into the gang.

The kid's name is Chris Decker, and we become

friends. He isn't much of a BMXer, but he surfs. I have a board, I tell him, and I'm down for going surfing. One weekend in May, Chris's dad, a big-time realtor in the area, has a meeting at the Oceanfront and agrees to drop us, along with another friend of Chris's, Brad Harrell, at the beach. Mr. Decker stuffs all three of our boards into the ample trunk of his Cadillac, and the butterflies in my belly take flight as we embark on my maiden session. Luckily, the meeting isn't near 1st Street, so I'm spared the potential embarrassment of searching for my sea legs in the middle of a crowd. In fact, we're all alone at the strip of beach where Mr. Decker drops us off.

May in Virginia Beach is warm, but the water remains chilly. I borrow a wetsuit and, as is often the case with newbies, put it on backward. Eventually, I get straightened out and join Chris and Brad in the water. They take turns riding some small but shapely waves, not only standing up but also angling down the line.

I watch and try to take it all in. Then, I give it a go, and I flounder. When you're 12, and motivated, you can learn anything. I manage to scratch into a few waves, each time pile-driving straight into the sand. I can hardly call what I do "surfing," but I catch a few waves and even ride one or two on my belly. The mission isn't an outright success, but I have accomplished two new things: I went to the beach without adult supervision and I rode my first wave.

The experience captivates me. From the prospect of going to the beach by ourselves, to the giddy anticipation of wondering what the waves will be like, to plunging "off the edge of the earth," to the dried salt on the back of my neck that sort of itches but that I don't want to wash off, the hook is set. And I haven't even stood up on a wave.

That summer, I spend more time at the beach than I have in my life, most of it at 1st Street. While certainly not a surf destination, Virginia Beach is a good place to pick up the fundamentals, especially from June through August. Sure, that's when the city caters to tourists, thus forcing the multitude of surfers into a clown car at 1st Street and the scant other designated surfing locations. However, when it comes to warm water and beginner-friendly waves, the summer months serve up a kook's cornucopia. The jetty at 1st Street gathers sand to form a consistent bar, producing a surfable wave nearly every day, so long as you don't mind the bumper-car atmosphere.

Surfing is a series of milestones, and that year I check off the first three: catching already-broken "whitewater" waves (which basically catch you rather than the other way around), getting to my feet, and eventually stroking into an unbroken wave. The last one is the game-changer. If surfing is nothing but riding whitewash, nobody would do it more than once or twice. Graduating from white-water to an actual wave equals the jump from crawling to walking. Either way, you're moving, but the difference is astronomical. At the risk of coming off as totally corn-ball, in that moment, you feel as if you're simultaneously harnessing nature and taking flight. The desire to re-create that feeling is what sends surfers on a never-ending journey from their first wave to their last.

JANUARY 2014

The first day of the year dawns frigid and flat. This is too easy. In January, our air and water temperatures in Virginia Beach hover around 40 degrees, and often plummet much lower. Most of the oceanfront tourist strip transforms into a ghost town. Aside from a few diehard joggers and the ever-present homeless populating the benches, the concrete boardwalk is tumbleweeds.

Just 364 more days like this—the year won't be a challenge at all. My schedule doesn't make it easy to surf on weekdays anyway, at least not with the shortened daylight of winter. It's either a dawn session before school or a mad dash to the beach before dark. But a few days later, the situation can't look more different.

At first, I debate whether to subject myself to wave checks, especially when I know there's surf. Maybe, I should avoid the sight of the ocean altogether, an impossible ask, I realize, given that you can see the ocean from my house. And, in summer, I'll still be running my surf school at the Oceanfront. Plus, Grady is surfing all the time, and watching him enjoy my beloved pastime makes me want to be out there even worse, adding further allure.

When I say you can see the ocean from my house, let me remind you that "my house" is actually the small apartment beneath my parents' home. My wife and my financial struggles left us unable to pay our mortgage, causing us to rent out our house and find more affordable accommodations. Luckily, my parents' apartment is available, so we throw most of our stuff into a storage unit and squeeze in downstairs. From their third-floor balcony, I can see across to the Atlantic. From our "basement," the view consists of overgrown bamboo and a wooden fence adorned with rusting tchochtkes.

I relish the novelty of pouring salt on my wound, and I decide to catch sight of as many waves as possible. By the first weekend of the year, I've had all the salt I can handle.

Everyone in the house is occupied come Saturday afternoon, so I hop on my bike for some exercise. It's chilly, but not enough to keep me indoors. I pedal from 62nd to 1st Street, gawking the whole time at beautiful, head-high waves. Normally, I'll do two surf sessions on a day like this, even in winter. *No big deal,* I convince myself as I pedal home. Besides, we're lucky to get good weekend waves once per month, so at least I won't have to endure more days like this for a while.

But damn if the following Saturday isn't 70 degrees with a building south swell, the kind of January day that brings out not just the hardcore crew but also the wannabes. People from all over flock to the Oceanfront to soak in the warmth. Then, they post selfies to make sure everyone knows they're living their best lives.

Aside from Smitty and my family, I haven't told anyone about my plan. I have every intention of documenting the experience in a journal, for posterity, but beyond that I don't want to make a big deal about it. The whole thing feels like a personal quest that not many people will be aware of while it's happening, but that I'll consider sharing when it's over. Apparently, January is a slow month for news in Virginia Beach, and the idea of keeping my plan incognito is almost immediately doomed.

By 10a.m. this Saturday, before my bike ride, my phone explodes with friends texting, "Have you checked anywhere?" and "What time you going out?" When there are waves, it goes without saying that surfers are going to surf. I respond to each query with, "Nah, I quit surfing." Seeing as how I've long ago earned a reputation as a smart-ass, it's understandable that people assume I'm messing with them. They eventually figure I had some family stuff to do, or that I discovered some secret North End spot and I'm refusing to divulge the goods, so they let it go. The truth, in fact, is beyond their comprehension.

When that Sunday dawns with more waves and even warmer weather, I'm ready to abandon ship. This isn't the Virginia Beach I know. My mind is accustomed to snapping into gear at the slightest hint of surf, scrolling through the forecast and tide charts to determine the optimal time for a session. Inside our apartment, I pace back and forth. Each time I look at my phone, time has barely moved. Rather than find a task to occupy my body and mind, I welcome the feeling of helplessness. I wanted to test my mettle, but I have to remind myself that something good will come of it. At least I hope so. I wonder if, somehow, someone is fucking with me.

The Indian Summer doesn't last, as a serious winter storm dumps snow on us the following weekend, enough to cancel school and bring the city to a standstill. And coastal snowstorms, in case you're unaware, are typically accompanied by wind and waves. Surfing in the snow isn't a big deal, but it presents a novel opportunity. Sessions get cut short as numbness tends to arrive quicker than on other days, but otherwise tromping across a snowy beach just adds to the adventure.

Cold hasn't stopped me from surfing in thirty years, ever since I first owned a decent wetsuit. While non-surfers bundle up indoors, feet on the ottoman and hot cocoa in hand, I relish zipping up and sprinting seaward. Sometimes I only nab a few waves before the inevitable pain spreading up from the fingers and toes to eventually become unbearable—chases me back to shore. By the time I get to my car, the uncontrollable shaking makes it difficult to unlock the door and start the ignition. When I was younger, and the wetsuit technology hadn't evolved to where it is today, it was even worse. I'd jump straight into a hot shower after a session, causing my fingers to sting with pain and then swell like fat sausages as the blood returned. Waves are a rarity, never to be taken for granted, so these minor inconveniences come with the territory.

Now, for the fourth time in just the first three weeks of the year, I'm faced with legitimate surf. But this time, I stare again at a lively Atlantic and just shrug. I will never forgive myself if I give up so quickly, so I need to learn how to deal with it. I resign myself to my new normal. I go home and boil some water for hot cocoa, put my feet on the ottoman, and rejoice in the warmth.

I figure it's time to let my brother in on my mission. He's full of ideas, and he isn't shy about sharing them. When I think back, it seems his favorite saying is anything starting with "You should..." As his younger brother, I was wired to assign more value to his suggestions than they likely warranted, like he was the all-knowing Yoda and I the fledgling Jedi. When Derrick hears what I'm doing, his first comment is, "You should do a blog about it." I've never read a blog and haven't considered writing one, but, as usual, his idea makes perfect sense—to me.

By the next day, I finish writing my initial post, entitled, "I quit." To add suspense, I make it sound as if I'm talking about getting divorced rather than quitting surfing, that I'm leaving my wife rather than taking a hiatus from riding waves, before finally revealing the truth. "How Surfing Ruined My Life" seems like a fun, tongue-in-cheek name for the blog, so I set it up and locate the 'post' button. Hardly anyone knows what I'm doing, so I can still conceivably shut my laptop and paddle out that very day. It could all go away, just like that. But clicking 'post' means I am committed. By this point, Derrick has signed off on the idea, and so I have no doubts.

Seeing as how most of the people who know me equate me with surfing, I expect my friends to be surprised when they catch wind of the plan. Like that article said, surfers don't walk away from surfing, especially not the hardcores whose very existence is so heavily tied to the sport. Still, the reception my post receives is a shock.

I have never left a flaming bag of shit on somebody's front porch (although I'd watched Derrick do it). But judging from some of the reactions to my post within the first twenty-four hours, I feel as if I've done just that. And I'll admit, watching people stomp in flaming crap is exhilarating.

To begin with, some miss the fact that the title is tongue-in-cheek: "I can't believe that someone like Jason Borte, a surfer I have always admired, would say that surfing ruined his life." Commenters are irate that I've decided to stay out of the water for a while. They rush to the defense of surfing, or how good my life is, or how bad their life is, or, to be honest, I don't know what they're defending, and I don't think they do either.

Fortunately, my critics take the time to express their dissatisfaction on that pillar of intelligent discourse, Facebook, so that others can pile on as well. In comment after comment, they bitch about not wanting to "hear someone bitch."

The most outraged of the bunch is a dude whose surfing I grew up admiring, one of the best to ever come out of Virginia Beach. Unfortunately for him, he's had a much harder go at life than I, compounding the tragedy that he missed the lecture on irony in English class that day. Probably out surfing.

In my initial post, I mentioned that I've made around a million dollars from surfing. My attacker comments, "I bet he's never had to empty his change jar to eat," failing to realize that the million bucks was spread over twenty-plus-years, making my average annual income from surfing less than my teaching salary. And, being the sole provider for a family of five, I'm well acquainted with scraping the change jar.

The Australian blogger Stu Nettle (swellnet.com) seems to understand where I'm headed. "Rather than playing superficial dress-ups, he's delving much deeper into his identity, both as a surfer and as a person," he writes, "and he's taking the path of most resistance to get there." Nettle claims it's an admirable task and wonders if he could do it—"take a yearlong vow of abstinence and shock my system into feeling."

Some of Nettle's readers agree, but many are somewhat less complimentary. They call me a "twit" and "the worst kind of self-indulgent wank." One suggests, "He must have some unresolved issues with himself," while another urges, "Spare us the blog and go break a leg instead."

Other commenters write lengthy rebuttals suggesting that I'm making the biggest mistake of my life, or that, once the weather changes, I'll be right back in the water. On the other hand, I receive a substantial number of comments depicting real interest in my pursuit. Either way, my misery now has an audience, and there is no turning back.

1983

Autumn supposedly lasts three months, same as all the other seasons, but that's bullshit. In Virginia Beach, we experience pleasant fall weather for a couple weeks, tops. Prior to that brief period of bliss, we are humidity's little bitch. There's a short respite come October, just long enough to catch a whiff of that crispy fall air, what Truman Capote dubbed "ideal apple-eating weather." Then, just as we begin to think, 'The climate's actually kinda nice around here,' Old Dude Winter sweeps down and smashes the dream.

Which is exactly what happens after my first summer of surfing. I do my best to cobble together enough rubber to fend off the chill, but it's of no use. The few times I make it to the beach bundled in a secondhand wetsuit, gloves, booties, and hood, I'm stiffer than Ralphie's little brother in *A Christmas Story*. On the few lines of whitewater I manage to catch, I fail to make it up to my feet. Any skills I've gained vanish under all that bulk.

To make matters worse, Derrick joins his high school wrestling team, leaving me no choice but to follow suit at Lynnhaven Middle School. Of course, my school's team hasn't lost a match in something like ten years, so this is no casual outing in the mat room. Coach Gary Hartranft takes out his frustrations at having such an inordinate ratio of consonants to vowels in his last name by putting us through ridiculous daily workouts. And, if he feels we're slacking off, he calls for a "red flag day," which is akin to the lifeguard signal for rough surf. Like a bunch of tourists getting our asses handed to us by pounding waves, we suffer under coach's fury. Ninety minutes of running, push-ups, sit-ups, crabwalks, and more running leaves me wondering why I'm not at the beach.

I'm second-string all season, so I never once wrestle in an actual match. Considering how much I fear the prospect of having to wear one of those tight, little singlets that so cruelly highlights one's tiny, seventh-grade package, I don't mind sitting in the bleachers. I've always enjoyed wrestling with Derrick and my dad around the house, but I soon realize the sport isn't for me. Secretly, I wish for our team's winning streak to end, but we, or I should say *they*, go on to another city championship. Wrestling, for me, is finished, as is the notion of working out.

In school, my interest in academics continues to wane as surfing occupies more and more of my thoughts. I begin seventh grade in "Superior" English but soon realize reading things like *The Odyssey* and *Beowulf* requires more work than I'm willing to do. After failing the first quarter, I convince my parents I'm out of my league and need to switch. They're both ultra-supportive of all our endeavors, but they don't demand much of us. We're offered cash for good grades on report cards, yet not enough to make much of a difference. I'm barely halfway through grade school, and my academic achievements are all behind me.

As my coursework lags, my efforts to belittle my teachers and classmates escalate. For whatever reason, I find that heckling others makes me feel really good about myself. I pretend to like unpopular girls until I earn their trust, and then tell them I'm kidding. I run my mouth off to teachers to get laughs, but I never push my luck far enough to get in trouble. What I deserve is an old-fashioned ass-kicking, but what I get from my peers is positive reinforcement.

As spring break approaches, Derrick presents my parents with information on an upcoming bus trip to Florida. The trip is being put on by 17th Street Surf Shop, whose owners my parents went to high school with. Here is an opportunity for Derrick to shed his wetsuit and enjoy some toasty waves, and since they're packing forty guys on a Greyhound and squeezing them into a crappy motel, the cost is affordable. He can talk my parents into things almost as easily as he can me, so they quickly sign off on it. "If he's going," I implore, "can I go, too?"

Sending an assertive 15-year-old (Derrick) on a surf trip is one thing, but a shy 12-year-old (me) offers reason for pause. Now, as a parent, I can understand thinking, "Hell yeah, we can get rid of both of them for the whole week." Whatever their thought process, they figure with Derrick along I'll be fine, so I'm soon booked on my first big surf adventure.

The bus is packed with the best surfers from around town, many of whom will be competing in the prestigious Easter Surfing Festival at Canaveral Pier alongside Florida's finest. I'm not among the best surfers anywhere and won't have anything to do with the contest. Hell, I haven't stood up on a wave in over six months. I spend the entire overnight trek down I-95 reminding myself of this fact, wondering what might happen when we hit the water. The other surfers are all nice enough on the bus, but how will they treat me when I'm exposed as a full-fledged kook?

At dawn, we pull up at a spot in Cocoa Beach called Second Light. The waves are barely two feet high, but the entire bus spills out in a mad dash to retrieve the boards from down below. As with any surf trip, there's no such thing as lounging upon arrival. Extended travel leaves you feeling as if you're covered in a layer of grime, and there's no better way to wash it off than by jumping straight into the ocean.

My fears of being revealed as a kook are fortunately unfounded, as the freedom of wearing nothing but a bathing suit allows me to stand on my first wave. Determined to make up for all that I've missed out on since the previous summer, I catch any scrap of wave that comes near me. Between rides, I study the more experienced guys and set about closing the vast performance gap. And, convinced that the water provides ample coverage for my pale, winterized body, I don't bother to wear sunscreen.

The next morning, we pull up at the Canaveral Pier

to check out the contest site, and what we see makes our competitors want to get back on the bus and drive home. On the very first wave, we witness a local take off, generate some down-the-line speed, and boost a 360-degree aerial. I've seen a lot of good surfing the previous day from VB's finest, but this is some futuristic shit.

Historically speaking, Virginia Beach ranks as high as anywhere on the East Coast in terms of importance within the sport. One of the first people to ride a wave along the Eastern Seaboard was a guy named "Big" Jim Jordan, whose uncle brought a 9' redwood surfboard back to VB after a visit to Hawaii sometime around 1912. Later, the early local lifeguard crew built lifesaving boards that performed double duty riding waves, and in the '60s, the city took over hosting the East Coast Surfing Championships, the longest-running surf competition in the United States. And by the early '80s, our place on the map is cemented by a lanky 6'4" Virginian named Wes Laine.

My friends and I refer to Laine as "OMG, it's Him." OMG Wes ranks among the Association of Surfing Professionals world tour's coveted Top 16 alongside guys from Australia, Hawaii, South Africa, and California. His reputation on tour is that of a heavy-water charger who is über consistent and, with his ridiculously long arms, an absolute paddling machine. Strangely enough, no one from Florida at this time can claim status in the elite Top 16. But, much like the NASA test pilots who broke barriers at nearby Cape Canaveral in the '50s and '60s, they have a bunch of flyboys intent on reaching the stars, including an 11-year-old named Kelly Slater.

A couple of our guys make their way to the finals in the event, but they can't hang with Kelly, his brother Sean, and the rest of the progressive Cocoa Beach contingent. The pro division is won by Matt Kechele, a surfboard shaper and local surf star. As for me, I neglect to wear sunscreen all week, so I'm a five-foot-tall walking blister. I haven't been exposed to much competition surfing, but I spend an entire day recuperating in the shade of the pier and taking in all the action. After a few days of striving to hang with the VB crew, and watching the East Coast's best do battle at the Easter Surfing Festival, I plan to test my skills in local competitions back at home.

The bus ride north bears no resemblance to the ride down. I came come down knowing nobody but Derrick, but now I'm on a "Hey, what's up?" basis with VB royalty, and I can even say I'm friends with a few of them. The sunburned skin that sloughs away in chunks all over my bus seat is that of a kid who no longer exists, a kid fumbling to find his place in the world. I'm still on the periphery, but I am becoming one of the boys.

Surf trips, I will soon discover, tend to follow a familiar pattern. They begin with excitement but uncertainty, and a burning need to prove oneself. On the return trip, there's always the satisfaction of a belly full of waves, challenges met, new friends made, and lots of peeling skin. And, strangely, I always look forward to diving back into 1st Street mayhem.

I'm a month away from my thirteenth birthday, and I

know what I want to do with the rest of my life.

The summer of 1982 was the best summer ever, but the 1983 version blows that one out of the water. Each summer, it seems, is better than the last. The difference is freedom. With every passing year, my world expands exponentially. I've survived a surf trip 800 miles from home, so my parents offer no protest to me biking 5 miles alone to 1st Street. Suddenly, I'm no longer dependent on anyone. I can wake up before dawn, grab my board, and pedal into the darkness toward my magical place, as if I'm slipping through the wardrobe into Narnia.

When you're 13, 5 miles is a long way to carry a surfboard while riding a bicycle, even a shortboard. I soon solve this issue with a hand-me-down board rack that I attach to my BMX bike. I look forward to an end to my struggles, as, the very next morning, I'll be cruising along Easy Street all the way to the beach. In fact, the night before, I'm so excited that I go in the garage and attach my board, another used model but a definite upgrade from the borrowed one, so I won't have to fumble with it at 5 a.m.

The next morning, I scarf down a bowl of Lucky Charms and hop on my bike. I roll out of the driveway and turn the corner. As soon as I do, the rack, which connects to my rear axle and holds my board aloft, comes loose. The tail of my board smashes into the pavement, where it grinds along for several feet until I reach a complete stop. So much for an easy ride. I'm not about to waste precious surf time dealing with the problem, so I go back to lugging my board.

Two summers removed from a gangster's paradise in Green Run, I'm now living in an actual paradise. Sure, I can't get my board rack to cooperate, but I've discovered the ultimate natural playground and have the freedom to come and go as I please. There's no entrance fee, no rulebook, and no limits to how much fun I can have even if the waves are crappy.

And that's just when I'm surfing. Between sessions, there are surf shops to hang out in, junk food to devour, and an endless procession of tourists who traveled here from far and wide to be heckled by the local punks. To me, the question isn't 'Why are there so many surfers out here?' but 'Why isn't *everyone* doing this?'

FEBRUARY 2014

I'm not the first East Coast teacher/writer to embark on some long, stupid, philosophical quest. Henry David Thoreau beat me to it by about 170 years. He, too, sought out a challenge that would give him insights into society, or a better understanding of himself, or at least something worthwhile to write about.

I paid no attention to Thoreau when my twelfth-grade English teacher blathered on about him, nor do I think of him when I embark on my own version of "life in the woods." But upon further review, I see that our motivations are similar: "I wished to live deliberately," Thoreau writes in *Walden,* "to front only the essential facts of life, and see if I could not learn what it had to teach, and not, when I came to die, discover that I had not lived." He claims he wanted "to conduct an experiment: could he survive, possibly even thrive, by stripping away all superfluous luxuries, living a plain, simple life in radically reduced conditions?" Likewise, my mission is nothing if not a reduction of the "radical."

Thoreau had his share of detractors who considered him a kook, and very few people purchased during his lifetime the book he wrote about his experience. He wouldn't live long enough to see himself revered as a philosopher, much less required reading across every high school in America. At 44, he ventured out during a late-night rainstorm to count tree rings and contracted bronchitis, later dying of complications. Sounds like an idiotic thing to do, yet a rainstorm never kept me from heading out for a few waves.

What strikes me about Thoreau's experiment is that he sought to gain a better understanding of society by getting away from it. Despite living through the horrible '80s rock ballad "Don't Know What You Got (Till It's Gone)" by the hair band Cinderella, I haven't thought of that angle. I honestly don't expect to gain a greater understanding of surfing, or my relationship with it, by quitting. I don't know what to expect.

During the first week of February, after days of being snowed in, I develop a wicked case of cabin fever. A sunny, 65° day is just what I need. Hudson and I bike to a playground on the beach.

While my boy scurries about the apparati like a hamster on a wheel, I notice a single longboarder bobbing alone in the sea. There aren't supposed to be any waves, but that never stops people from paddling out and just sitting there. After a few minutes, I spot a tiny right, peeling seamlessly along the sandbar offshore. And then another.

The swell, what little there is of it, is from the south, just the way I like it. South swells equal long, right-breaking waves, which, as a regularfoot (left-foot-forward surfer), are tailor-made for me. This spot, I recall, comes alive on a south swell, so much so that a few friends and I refer to it as "The Superbank," after the famed right-hand pointbreak along Australia's Gold Coast.

A memory pops into my brain of another day here, nearly a year earlier to the day. I called out sick from school, but I still mustered enough energy to surf perfect barrels, an absolute rarity around here, with only a few other people. Due to my "weakened condition," I was only able to surf for about five hours in total. The waves, meanwhile, held out until dark.

This day looks identical, only the waves are six inches rather than six feet. Still, I'm mesmerized by their impeccable shape. I immediately lose myself in a reverie, mentally shrinking down to action-figure size and threading in and out of the flawless tubes. Since it's all in my mind, I don't stop with merely getting barreled, instead capping each ride with a massive, spinning aerial.

I don't remember when during my youth I quit seeing waves as karate targets and began instead imagining them as my own personal racetracks, but it was soon after I started surfing. Gradually, I became physically unable to see any breaking wave without mind-surfing it. The same goes for any surfer. I wonder if, at some point this year, I might look at a wave and see nothing but a wave. Do I want that moment to occur, or will it mean that I'm dead inside? And am I breaking my own rules by riding these waves in my mind?

Either way, I enjoy it, so I keep going. Midway through another epic ride, I hear, "Dad, did you see that?" It's my son, excited over nearly traversing the monkey bars.

"What, huh? No, I missed it, buddy." Pissed at being pulled from my daydream, I grumble, "Do it again." My mindsurf session only lasts a few minutes, but it provides a satisfaction similar to having actually surfed. The guy on the longboard isn't catching any waves, but I score perfection without having to step foot in the water.

A week later, driving home from work, I cross the Rudee Inlet Bridge, which offers an elevated view of 1st Street. Dusk is approaching, but I can clearly make out the lineup. And as far as I can see, the waves are pumping. I peel around the corner at the bottom of the bridge and hightail it down to get a closer look. Around here, when you catch a glimpse of a real wave, you haul ass to the beach without thinking. As I stand half in and half out of my car on the boardwalk, my gaze meets nothing but head-high, glassy rights stacked one after another.

It will take more than these six weeks so far to undo thirty-plus years of conditioning, so I instinctively turn toward the back of my car to see if my board and wetsuit are there. There's just enough light left to rush out and get a wave or two. But in the fraction of a second it takes to snap my head around, the blow has been delivered.

Oh yeah, I don't surf.

Somehow, I'm not bummed. As soon as I release the sense of urgency that comes with seeing good waves on the East Coast, it is replaced with a weird sense of calm. I'm less than two months into my experiment, and it feels like something positive has already come from the endeavor.

While I'm not stressing about missing waves, I try to remember if this much surf is normal. Five days of legitimate waves in only six weeks? In Virginia Beach? This is out of the ordinary, more than double what I've come to expect. And then I realize that, maybe, just maybe, there is such a thing as a surf god, and I've turned myself into a human sacrifice.

I attended a surf sacrifice back in 1984, the night before an ESA. contest at 1st Street. We torched some guy's dilapidated board in a trash can in hopes of appeasing the gods enough to send waves for the event. The next morning, the board was burnt to a crisp, but the ocean remained dead flat. Perhaps, releasing a bunch of foam and resin chemicals into the atmosphere wasn't the best way to satisfy the gods.

According to Australian surf mythology—in which the gods are slightly less famous but far more raucous and foul-mouthed than those on Mt. Olympus—the surf is controlled by a god named Huey. And Huey, for some reason, despises America's East Coast, perhaps not as much as he loathes the Gulf Coast or Great Lakes, but what can you expect from a gulf and some lakes?

My refusal to surf, apparently, appeases Huey, so he's rewarded Virginia Beach with an inordinate amount of surf, at least by our standards. Oftentimes, our actions carry negative unintended consequences, so if my experiment has benefitted the other surfers in town, that's reason enough to keep it going. Besides, they'll owe me a few waves when I eventually return to the lineup.

1984

I can't stand small talk, so there must be some other reason I gravitate toward 1st Street. There are other options where one can give up a bit of wave quality for some valuable social distancing. For me, a raging introvert, there's never a question. On rare occasions, I surf somewhere else in town, but 1st Street becomes my adopted home.

My acceptance of the madness may have something to do with football, and baseball, and karate, and BMX, and growing up with an older brother. The spirit of competition is in me from the beginning. In the '80s, longboards are hard to come by at any beach aside from the cruisiest, so during my formative years nobody has a built-in advantage when it comes to catching waves. Most everyone rides a board that is not much taller than they are. Therefore, a system of determining who-gets-what-wave is required, and that system is known as the "pecking order." The most skilled and experienced surfers have their pick of the best waves, and everyone else fights for the leftovers.

As a young beginner, I'm at the bottom of the totem pole. I sit closer to shore and wait for whatever tiny waves make it past OMG Wes (when he's in town), followed by his buddies, followed by the teenaged hotshots, followed by the older kooks, followed by the other young grommets. Soon enough, I at least have a shot against the other kids and older kooks. Girls are a rarity in most lineups, an unfortunate fact that won't change until well into the '90s.

Surfing as a sport is experiencing a time of rapid growth, with a burgeoning professional tour and multiple thriving amateur organizations through which funnel the future pros. Companies that started in guys' garages during the '70s are now selling hundreds of millions of dollars in surfwear and moving into massive corporate offices around Southern California. With their ever-growing marketing budgets, they hold events and sponsor surfers all over the world. There is competition everywhere: among companies over market share, among pros for money and ratings points, among amateurs for exposure and sponsorships, and among surfers at 1st Street and every other spot for waves.

I'm immersed in this wonderful, natural pursuit—riding waves—and it's all I want to do. Because of where I surf, and where in the sport's evolution I happen to come along, the competitive aspects are inextricable from the inherent beauty. I want to be higher in the pecking order, so I can catch better waves; to accomplish that, I must surf better. No one else cares if my surfing improves—nobody but me. There's no team, no one relying on me to work together for a common goal of winning. I want it. I need it. I push myself, and I enjoy every moment of it.

One summer day at 1st Street, a VW bus pulls up sporting Florida plates. We all eye the vehicle suspiciously, as this isn't something that happens every day. Out steps a thin, curly-haired driver and two rather dark, square-shouldered groms. At any spot, this crew is instantly recognizable: Matt Kechele, the guy we'd watched win the Easter Surfing Festival in Cocoa Beach the previous year, along with his even more famous proteges, Sean and Kelly Slater.

The guys are midway through a two-week tour promoting Sundek, a Florida surfwear company that sponsors the trio, passing out stickers and catching some waves along the way. While these gator boys may have stepped out of their van and onto welcome mats at other spots along the coast, this isn't the case at 1st Street. Through years of osmosis, we've received the memo from our local elders: it's us against the intruders. For the first time, I feel the peach fuzz on my back stand at attention.

For the record, with OMG Wes away on tour, there is only one local with anything resembling the skill of any of these three, and that's Pete Smith, Jr. The son of an OG VB legend, Pete is 16 and (unfortunately) at the peak of his career. He is no less talented than Kelly Slater, but with none of the freakish drive that would see the Floridian rewrite surfing history. Instead, Pete will drop out of school, burn whatever brain cells he has left, and, without the charity of the owners of 17th Street Surf Shop, join our local homeless population.

Regardless of our obvious talent deficit, or the fact

that the waves this day are barely knee high, it's our jetty, and we have to defend it. I latch onto Sean Slater, who is closest to my age, and make it my mission to outdo him. The visitors are as nice as they can be, but it seems it is my job to refuse their Sundek stickers and try to keep them from catching any of "our" waves. As laughable as this all seems now, when I see that van pull away, I have the feeling that We've won.

Spending my days in the 1st Street gladiator pit, it's inevitable that I'll try my luck in surf contests. In fact, I already competed in a few events the previous summer in the 12-and-under "Menehune" division. In addition to a few contests in town, I traveled with Chris Decker and his mom to Hatteras for an ESA event. Chris bonked his head and got a concussion, and I reached the finals. By 1984, I'm surfing year-round and consistently making finals, and sometimes winning, in the 13- to 14-year-old Boys Division.

Derrick, for his part, isn't finding much success. He's good enough to advance through a heat or two, but in the highly competitive 14–17 Juniors Division, the opposition is too strong. Rather than take out his frustration on me, which would be understandable, he becomes my biggest supporter, using his evil genius to convince those in the industry that, if they're smart, they'll sponsor his little brother.

As much as I love winning, and being better than Derrick at something for once, I never feel as if I go surfing to improve. Surfing is fun, every aspect of it. The getting up at 5 a.m., the joking with friends on the way to the beach, the anticipation of pulling up at the boardwalk to check the waves, the sneaky maneuvering in the lineup to get in the best position, the studying how some guys generate speed despite the weak conditions, the creative harassment of tourists along Atlantic Avenue, the anxious turning of the pages of a new surf magazine, the stripping off an old coat of wax and applying a fresh bar for that perfect traction, the graceful dismount onto the sand after connecting all the dots from the takeoff, and mostly, the knowledge that I'll be doing it all over again tomorrow.

Occasionally, I get dropped off at the beach, and as it gets close to sunset, I realize I don't have my bike or any way home. Such is the case after a day of particularly good waves in May of that year. The parking lot has mostly emptied, and the only guy I know is a friend of Derrick's whom I've met just once. Jeff Hunter is a good surfer who also lives pretty far from the beach. It's his sixteenth birthday, and he's inherited his brother's old Dodge Colt. Looking to flex his fresh driver's license, which he received just that day, he jumps at the opportunity to give me a ride home. From that moment on, Jeff and I are the best of friends—and the best of rivals.

MARCH 2014

I recall a day not too long ago when I was surfing at the North End, and a guy around my age paddled out. The man insisted on making small talk, and after missing a few waves and blowing the takeoff on some others, he felt the need to express that he knew he was a kook, and he didn't care. "It's about the process," he babbled. "I just do it for the exercise." As I read more angry comments from my detractors, incensed that I'm taking time away from the water, I think of "Process Guy." And it pisses me off.

His approach, surfing for mere exercise, like it's nothing more than running or going to the gym, is reprehensible, blasphemous even. I'm furious. He's taken surfing—this glorious communion with nature—and diminished it into CrossFit.

By my third month of self-imposed exile, I get around to exploring the reasons I surfed. My quickly scribbled list of reasons goes like this: fun, camaraderie, and to escape from any number of life's complexities. Compare that to the motives for taking a spin class, or any other physical activity for that matter, and while the fun part may get knocked down a few pegs, there really isn't much of a difference. As it turns out, Process Guy had a point.

There are aspects within surfing that you don't find in other pursuits, but our reasons for doing it, or in my case not doing it, are our own. For so long, I believed that what I was doing was beyond special, that nothing on Earth could compare to riding waves, and the 99.7 percent of humans who don't do it are wasting their lives. Surfing became my default mindset as opposed to a conscious choice: if I'm grabbing my board and going to the beach just because it's what I do, I'm not giving it any more respect than Process Guy.

There's only one person I know who is more conditioned to surf than me, and that's my friend Ken Hunt.

Ken rides basically the same boards, sports the same flawless Ken-doll hairdo, cracks the same corny jokes, and quotes the same raunchy movies he did back when Reagan was president. Ken gets in the water as often as anyone, logging an "obligatory" session on days that others wouldn't even consider. There was no way he'd understand what I was doing, so I avoided telling him. When he heard, he hit me with a barrage of texts: "Do I need to do an intervention?" "Live for today." "You have a gift." "Inspire the youth." When those each proved fruitless, he came with the heavy artillery: "If our old friends who are no longer with us could speak with you today, they'd tell you to stop being so silly and catch a wave for them!"

Eventually, I decide to let Ken think he's won: "Okay, let me know when you're surfing," I text him. "I'm in."

A few hours later, he calls. "The good news is, there's nobody out at 1st Street," he says. "The bad news is, that's because there's nothing to entice them. Actually, there's a little wave, and the tide's pushing in. It's time; let's rock and roll."

Ken is a full Type-A-personality salesman for Billabong clothing, among the best in the surf industry. He keeps his salesmanship sharp by talking his friends into accompanying him for his daily half-hour session. We call it "Getting Kenned" when he convinces us to paddle out in absolute crap. And while, on the surface, it seems the reason is that misery loves company, Ken is never miserable when he's surfing. For him, I think it really is about the process. As long as he can climb to his feet and go down the line, he's stoked.

I pull up at the jetty and see that he's "Kenned" one other sucker. While they both struggle to get going on a wave, I squeeze into my hooded five-millimeter suit, gloves, and boots, giggling the entire time.

Ken doesn't see me until I'm waist deep in icy Atlantic water. A wave of excitement (easily the wave of the day) washes over him when he sees that he's "saved" me from wasting a year of my life. The feeling vanishes just as quickly when he notices that I have no surfboard. I wade into the 38° water carrying nothing but the smile on my face.

He pushes his board toward me. "Come on, dude, it's good for the soul," Ken says. But I'm immune to his sales tactics. I hang out for a few minutes, swim around a bit, and make sure to check off all the boxes from my list of reasons for surfing, without ever riding a wave. I even give Ken a helpful shove to get going on one. It's the fastest his board moves all session.

I love Ken and respect his dedication to surfing, but I can't fathom how fighting to churn out some forward momentum and eking out a turn on the closeout a few times each day can benefit anybody's soul. Watching him rhythmically pump down the line as if chugging up a track on one of those railroad handcars, I flash on the notion that surfing puts him into some kind of mindless, meditative trance. I see him as The Little Engine That Could, all the while chanting the internal mantra, "I think I Ken, I think I Ken, I think I Ken."

Could that be part of surfing's grip, the repeated spurts of erasing the mental static, a form of athletic meditation? For guys like Ken, whose minds are always working overtime, those precious seconds may be the only reprieve in the course of a hectic day. In that regard, riding waves equally benefits the body and the mind. Either way, for me, stepping out for a few laughs with my friends, like we were still teenagers, is good for my soul. I feel as if I've surfed.

On the second weekend in March, much of the East Coast scores clean overhead waves, another reeling south swell. Ugh! And other than my walk into the lineup at 1st Street, I haven't entered the water. In need of some exercise, I decide to give the rec-center pool a try.

Others apparently have the same idea. I have to share a lane with a girl who might be training for the Olympics. Back and forth, back and forth. Damn, it's boring. And on top of the tedium, the chlorine burns my eyes. I keep pace with my lane mate for three or four lengths, but I'm exhausted. The bitch laps me, not once but several times.

After half an hour, I sit on the side of the pool to catch my breath. As the girl makes her turn beside me, she shoots me a sideways glare that seems to say, "Out of my lane, you pitiful old wuss."

In the shower, I accidentally see some guy's saggy ball-sack, or is that my own in the mirror? It isn't, but he's me in twenty more years, another blink of the eye.

Daylight savings is due to begin. It's a moment I've forever cherished, first as a kid who had to return home when the streetlights turned on, and especially now as a middle school teacher who works until 4 p.m. So, I have that to look forward to, until I realize that another hour of daylight is no longer in my best interest. I'm truly a fish out of water.

Before I can escape the month, the surf god Huey has one more surprise in store. On the final weekend of March, we have to attend school on Saturday to make up for all the snow days We've missed. Sitting in a classroom on a weekend feels wrong, like that moment when you realize you're listening to a Nickelback song on the radio, but for the whole day. When I'm not working, I've been handling all the household chores while Mrs. B finishes her final months of nursing school and helps transition her grandmother into a nursing home.

That Sunday morning, after the kids and dogs have

eaten and the last load of laundry is in the dryer, my phone lights up with a text from Ken: "Any chance you would go to the Outer Banks with me today?" He isn't trying to "Ken" me this time; he's offering to drive me to Hatteras to ride perfect barrels with him, which may as well be Hugh Hefner sending his chauffeur to drive you to a party in your honor at the Playboy Mansion.

Instead, I reply with, "No thanks, buddy. Maybe next year." I used to wish for the surf to turn to crap whenever I couldn't be out there, but for the first time in my life, I genuinely want my friends to score good waves, even without me. I pull up the surf cam later that day and text Ken a screenshot of a beautiful, empty wave, hoping he's somewhere in the vicinity.

"Nice," he responds, "after I decided not to go. I'm such a kook." As much as I wish success for my boys, I don't mind hearing that my misery also has some company.

1985

Thanks to YouTube, we take videos for granted. We can watch anything, anytime. In 1985, my family had a Betamax, the videocassette- format that eventually lost out to VHS. Finding surf movies in Beta format was a challenge. All I'd been able to watch at home were a couple bad 1970s surf flicks that my mom picked up at the video store. Ninety minutes of slow-motion Pipeline was more a cure for insomnia than a way to get pumped to surf 1st Street. One day, I follow Derrick into a new surf shop in town, and everything changes.

Island Water Sports is run by a guy straight out of the '70s, Scott Burdette. Scott has a bushy mustache, a pot belly, a pack-a-day habit, a parrot named Maui that squawks at visitors, and endless stories of his days as a sales rep for the legendary surf company Lightning Bolt. The shop is dark and musty, and up on a shelf there's a VCR hooked to a TV no larger than a laptop screen. It's the perfect setting for watching slow-motion Pipeline on an endless loop, not someplace you'd expect to transport you into the future.

Anything filmed within the decade is considered state-of-the-art, but what I witness on that shitty screen is newer—less than a year old. *Off The Wall 2*, the first new surf flick released on VHS, features a guy named Davey Smith boosting some of the first aerials caught on film, but that's far too futuristic for my tastes. Another segment highlights a different California pro, Tommy Curren, riding his home break of Rincon. It's as close to a come-to-Jesus moment as I've ever experienced.

I've seen Curren in the magazines, but never in moving pictures. Here is the best surfer on Earth, exercising incomprehensible speed and power, yet flowing with the economy of movement of a Baryshnikov. I haven't given much thought to surfing style; I've always just hopped up and did what felt good. Suddenly, that changes. Everything I do, whether I'm skateboarding, riding my bike, holding my hand out the car window, or riding a wave, I aim to do it like Curren—with panache. Thousands of other surfers similarly try aping Curren's style, but my mimicry is more convincing than most. In the local contests, I go from being among the handful of kids capable of winning to pretty much dominating.

While I remain way down the pecking order in the lineup at 1st Street, my crew's reputation as smart-asses is unparalleled. Along with my buddy Jeff, I spent most of my time with two legendary jokesters, Jay McGovern and Brian "Woody" Woodruff. Between sessions, Jay and I hold court at Sea Level Surf Shop at the corner of 16th Street, which is a one-way road. Tourists often drive the wrong way up the street, and we'll run down from the shop porch and order them to turn around. Sure, they've already driven nearly the length of the block and are a scant few feet from turning onto another road, but we are adamant about upholding the law, or at least about having fun at their expense.

Woody specializes in coming up with original ways of freaking people out. One day at 1st Street, he suggests we stage a mock fight. We yell obscenities at one another and wrestle across every beach towel we can step on, knocking over as many beach chairs and coolers as we can reach. By the time we grow tired, we've kicked sand across three blocks of towels and left dozens of beachgoers wondering what the hell just happened.

Woody's favorite pastime is running up to a random stranger and yelling, "Uncle Pete, how ya' been?" He leans in to hug his stunned prey, who inevitably backs away and replies, "Huh? My name's not Pete. You got the wrong guy." That's when Woody kicks into another gear, coming back with, "What's the matter with you, Pete? You've changed, man. Wait until I tell dad about this!" He goes on like this for a while and then stomps away, leaving his victim in a state of confusion. It's a miracle that none of these people just knock him out.

For the first time, the ESA holds multiple regional qualifiers to whittle the ever-growing field down to a manageable contingent for the East Coast Championships. The inaugural Mid-Atlantic Regionals are set for Ocean City, Maryland, a two-hour drive to our north. Amid hotel pranks including fire-extinguisher battles, water-filled ice buckets propped above slightly opened doors, and lots of farting in faces, Ocean City provides us competitors with good waves, some of the best I've surfed in competition.

I place second in the Boys division. I should be happy with the result, but the kid who beats me, a country boy from North Carolina, sports a rat-tail and various bleached shapes in his hair. He looks like a complete idiot, but his ridiculous hairdo isn't what angers me the most—it's his complete disregard for style, as if he's never seen a Tom Curren video in his life. I'm baffled as to how the judges can reward his spastic, flapping approach. Before beginning my mission to become Mr. Smooth, it would have been nice to know that contest judges can be so easily swayed by a surfer who makes moves look more difficult than they actually are.

Competitive successes lead to ever-widening travels, and my regionals finish means I'm expected to represent the Virginia District in Cape Hatteras for the ESA Championships later this year. Hatteras is the perfect spot to hold this event, and not merely because it sits roughly halfway between Maine and Miami; the Outer Banks of North Carolina is also the epicenter for East Coast surf, and Hatteras, because it juts into the Atlantic, is open to receiving surf from several directions. Plus, the absence of a wide continental shelf means that the waves that hit its shore are chockful of power.

Hatteras is where OMG Wes capped off his stellar amateur career before heading onto the world tour years earlier, and where Kelly Slater, soon after his 1st Street session in 1984, got his first taste of real tube-riding. As a Virginia Beach surfer, I'm raised, rightly or not, to think of Hatteras as an extension of my backyard. Any time the wind turns offshore on a sizable swell, the 1st Street lineup regulars clear out and head south. The best surfers in the water during these forays are typically Wes or one of his disciples, indicating to me that I better learn how to ride a real wave.

Hatteras presents a learning curve as steep as the waves themselves, as I discover with my initial two Outer Banks adventures. The first, a couple years earlier, demonstrates how much I still have to learn about the weather. My dad promises to take Chris Decker and me on a summer surf mission, and he leaves it to me to let him know when the waves will be good. In the days before online surf forecasts, one has to make such calls on a regular basis. I know we need onshore winds to make waves, followed by offshore winds to clean them up. Based on that knowledge, I study the weather forecast in the newspaper daily, waiting for just the right conditions.

Finally, after I've spent weeks dutifully assessing the forecast, the wind is about to turn in our favor. I give my dad the go-ahead, and we grab Chris and hit the road. Two hours later, pumped full of candy and expectations, we pull up to the beach in Nags Head to find what looks like a lake. The ocean is completely flat aside from tiny ripples from the onshore wind.

Wait, *onshore?* I fail to realize that the wind direction isn't actually the direction the wind is blowing *toward,* but the direction it's coming *from*. So, after weeks of offshore (southwest) winds, we show up just as the wind turns onshore (northeast). Thankfully, my dad salvages the trip by taking us to the giant sand dune of Jockey's Ridge and a water flume. The next day back at 1st Street, I make the mistake of mentioning to an older kid that I'd gone to Hatteras. He says, "Me, too—it was epic, huh?" I think he's kidding, but he adds, "It was flat all the way to Buxton, but around the corner in Frisco it was offshore and barreling." I grit my teeth and say, "Yeah, it was good."

My second escapade south of the border comes on a family trip that happens to coincide with a big swell. It's way overhead, at least double the size of anything I've experienced at home, and twice as powerful. I see just how different Cape Hatteras is from 1st Street. At the Rodanthe Pier, I excitedly follow Derrick and a couple friends into the lineup, only to get beaten down and swept straight through the pilings. My dad, equipped with a new video camera and trying to capture the session from above, runs frantically atop the pier thinking he's going to have to dive in to rescue me. Fortunately, I miss the pilings and emerge from the other side unscathed. It takes me all morning to make it out to the lineup, and another couple hours of dodging real waves before I manage to grab a benign whitewater back to the beach.

Undeterred, I know from listening to my 1st Street elders that you either surf well in Hatteras or you're relegated to kook purgatory. Any time I hear someone mention taking a trip down south, I hop in for the ride, determined to adapt my small-wave game to surf of consequence. As much as I love navigating the circus at my home break, I'm infatuated with Hatteras. Instead of an overabundance of people in your way as you struggle to generate speed on a slow wave, the challenge here is handling the power. These waves pack a serious punch, and crowds are almost never a factor. Soon, I'm able to translate my small-wave skills to fit the steeper conditions, and there's nothing I enjoy more than a day trip with friends.

As soon as I learn to turn my board and garner a couple contest results, surf companies offer me sponsorship. In the beginning, that means a few stickers and a T-shirt. More importantly, it means guidance from others who have been where I want to go. My first sponsor is a clothing company called Norfleet. I've never heard of them, but the offer of a sticker for my board is too much to resist. The team is run by a VB surfer/waiter named Paul West, and he takes us all to Hatteras to stay in a pop-up trailer near the lighthouse for an ESA event.

The contest isn't memorable, but camping with a group of surfers for the first time is unforgettable. Having never encountered pot smoke, I'm faced with a pop-up hotbox all weekend. One evening before dark, a few of the younger guys trek to the beach and discover perfect, empty waves. A massive thunderstorm rolls through, but with no one around to order us out of the water, we surf right through the lightning. The area is notoriously infested with sharks, further adding to the adventure. We notice a few fins, but it'll take more than sharks and lightning bolts to pry us away. We surf until dark, and we vow not to tell our parents what We've done. I'm not sure Paul's lax supervision would meet my mom's standards.

By the time the ESA Championships roll around that September, I've logged a whole summer of successful Outer Banks strike missions. The waves for this massive event are fun but unintimidating. In the Boys Division, I slip through several heats to advance to the eight-person, man-on-man, double-elimination finals. There, I face a bevy of Floridians, including Kelly Slater. He's already won the event twice, as well as the U.S. Championships in Hawaii, but luckily, we're on opposite sides of the draw. We each win two more heats, meaning we're due to meet up in a match of unbeatens.

Kelly is head and shoulders above everyone, so to challenge himself he's been trying a sort of back flip (known as a barrel roll) on a few waves late in the heats. Just before paddling out for what I already know will be my beatdown, I turn to fellow Vah Beacher Brad Harrell and ask, "What if he does one of those flip things in our heat?" Brad shrugs and says, "I dunno—try one, too."

I drop anchor where I've seen the best waves coming in, and Kelly circles the lineup like a little brown shark. He finds the first wave, and I watch from behind as he bashes it once, then twice, before blasting well above the lip. Silhouetted upside down in front of the pristine dunes, he spares me much suffering by going straight for the kill. He flips his board all the way around, stands upright, and then continues riding toward the beach.

There's no good reason for me to catch any waves after seeing that, but I figure I'll at least be a good sport. It's the only heat in my life where I feel I shouldn't even be out there. I lose my next heat as well, leaving me in a respectable third place for the entire East Coast.

That night, back at the hotel where I'm staying with a friend and his older sister, I celebrate, as any 15-year-old would, with poker and vodka. At some point, the hotel manager joins in the game, and the last thing I remember is getting up from the table and puking all over the bed.

APRIL 2014

I consider myself lucky. Always have, but stepping away from surfing opens my eyes to how charmed my life has been. I haven't inherited a trust fund, wasn't born with any prodigious talents, and have yet to hit the lotto. However, when the toughest challenge I've faced, after four-plus decades of drawing breath on this planet, is refraining from riding a wave for a year, I have to wonder if there's a luckier human being anywhere. And if that's true, then am I also the most selfish?

In April, Virginia Beach shakes off the heft of winter. Most serious swells migrate toward the Southern Hemisphere with the change in weather, a fair tradeoff for water temps rising out of ice-cream-headache territory. Surfers shed their burdensome gloves and boots, swapping these out for congested lineups and parking meters.

Into my fourth month of "surf-briety," a time you'd expect my challenge to become unbearable, it's feeling just the opposite. I'm not pining for a few warm waves so much as being eaten away by guilt over all those I've already ridden, all the countries I've visited, all the checks I've cashed for doing so, and all the cards that stacked in my favor to make these things happen.

By dumb luck, I was born male and white, two key factors for an easy entry into surfing during the 1980s. There were scant few female surfers around town, no more than three or four whom I encountered. Of those girls who ignored the sport's gender barrier, many were branded as "butches" at a time when homosexuality was not socially accepted. In an attempt to maintain masculine hegemony over the lineup, male surfers afforded little to no respect to the fairer sex. There was a decent number of Asian-Americans in the VB lineup, but the Black contingent, in an area with a considerable Black population, could be counted on one hand. Cab Spates, a guy I went to school with, was among the best surfers in town, so it wasn't a question of any lack of ability. As enlightened as our residents think they are, racism remains a big issue today, and it was even bigger thirty years earlier.

There wasn't anything keeping me from going surfing. By the time I knew that such a thing existed, I was in an upper-middle-class household that was relatively close to the beach. Had my parents not been so supportive of whatever endeavors Derrick and I decided to try, or not had the money for my mom to be a housewife with the time to drive us all over town, who knows what we would've gotten into? Even when I biked to the beach, I wasn't confronted with gangs or drug dealers or any real dangers. The biggest threat to my well-being was potentially running my mouth off to the wrong lifeguard or tourist.

The first time I stepped foot outside the United States,

at age 17, some friends and I crossed the border from California to experience the mayhem of Tijuana. Immediately, we were besieged by bands of children selling packs of Chiclets gum. Failing to recognize the dire circumstances of these kids' lives, I haggled with them over the price of the gum, and then didn't buy any at all. The same evening, I'd be returning to a hearty dinner and a comfortable bed before getting up for another surf, while they were likely relegated to dirt floors, scraps, and potentially much worse. For years, I traveled to various surf destinations, all the while witnessing Third World despair. I'd done nothing to warrant my life of relative luxury, yet I turned a semi-blind eye to those who hadn't been so lucky.

Physically, I inherited a body type favorable for athletics (albeit without the height I needed for football or basketball). I had no serious physical or mental ailments, and enough intelligence to not get myself into any situations that I couldn't get out of. Still, my arrival on the surfing scene required good timing. Had I grown up in any other century, chances are I wouldn't have enjoyed such an inordinate amount of leisure time, short of being born into royalty. I might've been forced to work in a coal mine or factory or farm—or at least not had access to a small foam-and-fiberglass surfboard that I could carry to the beach when my bike rack broke.

Given these ridiculous built-in advantages, I still required heaps of 'in-the-moment' luck. There were many times I nearly blew it in an instant with a single dumb lane change on the road to Hatteras or a cheeky drop-in in front of an angry kook at 1st Street having an already-bad day. I took my advantages for granted, failing to appreciate what I'd been given. I reaped countless rewards from all those unearned windfalls and repeatedly paddled back out for more.

Realizing I've been selfish and a less-than-ideal human, I try to rationalize my behavior. Aren't *all* surfers selfish, always wanting more waves and fewer crowds? I'm one of them, so it's not my fault; I'm just wired this way. And sure, surfing is a healthful pursuit, good for the body and the mind, and maybe no more selfish than going to the gym. But who am I kidding? I *never* surfed for exercise—I was enjoying three sessions a day or flying away multiple times a year for a week of wave-filled bliss.

Considering the grip surfing has held over my life, and the amount that it has informed my actions for decades, I classify our relationship as somewhere between addiction and religion. Not to belittle the plight of addicts or the beliefs of devotees, but I don't see much of a difference. I could dissect the definition in either case, or use any parallels to minimize my own selfishness. But instead, having now lost my religion, I am able to view it from a clearer vantage point.

Stepping away from surfing enables me to see how next-level my selfishness has been, how I've lived a disgustingly fortunate but unexamined life, and how my priorities have to change. By my estimation, I owe a massive debt, but to whom? I've caught enough waves, reaped enough benefits. There has to be a way of repaying, or paying forward, what has been given to me. I don't know the answer, but I'm determined to find it.

Or, maybe it's just that I have too much idle time now. When my year is over, I'll probably forget all about it.

HIGH SCHOOL

There are two types of students: those who apply themselves to mastering the curriculum in preparation for college and a career, and those who show up every day out of nothing more than obligation. I'll give you one guess which of those two camps describes me. Throughout high school, only my senior English teacher leaves any sort of impression on me, and that's because he's hilarious. He tells us funny stories and offers extra credit for answering rock-and-roll trivia questions, such as 'How did Jimi Hendrix die?' (he choked on his own vomit) and 'What are two Simon and Garfunkel songs with the word "bridge" in them?' ("The 59th Street Bridge Song" and "Bridge Over Troubled Water"). I'm in school because I have to be.

The last book I read was in seventh grade: *The Twenty-One Balloons*. Surf magazines are my bible, and my notes are either caricatures of my teachers or wave doodles in the margins. Without paying attention or putting in much effort, I get by with mostly Bs and Cs. As long as I maintain Cs or better, my parents ask nothing of me and continue to feed my surfing habit. My mom washes, dries, and folds my laundry, and a hot dinner is served every night. When the waves are exceptionally good, she lets me skip school.

My travels prior to high school have taken me only along the East Coast. Our trips have been drives in the family station wagon to Disney World or New York for a cousin's bat mitzvah. With no formal training, my dad decides to try designing and building custom homes. He quickly gains a reputation as being among the best in the area, and his newfound successful career means we can afford to see more of the world. Surfing consumes Derrick's and my lives, so my parents plan family trips around waves.

After my run in the ESA Championships, I'm chosen as a member of the ESA All-Star Team. Most of the team is from Florida, so they're able to feed off one another in the water on a regular basis. The only gathering of the entire team is an event in 1986 in Ventura, California, where we will compete against the West Coast All-Stars. My parents make a vacation out of it, dragging my sister along and renting a house outside Los Angeles.

Before we leave, our local paper, *The Virginian-Pilot,* interviews me for an article in their twice-weekly Virginia Beach insert called "The Beacon." The headline boasts, "Teenage surfer heads for championships." In it, I'm described as a "cross between Steve Martin and Howdy Doody," but serious about surfing. Our ESA director, an older resident surfer, is quoted as saying, "[H]e's in that core group of the twenty or thirty best surfers in Virginia Beach." People can call me Howdy Doody all they want, but when I read the "twenty or thirty" comment, I'm insulted. I'm barely 16, have been surfing for just four years, but I know that there aren't even a dozen local guys better than me, much less twenty or thirty. Every contest, every session, every wave, I compare myself to other surfers, methodically assessing my abilities against the brightest talent around. My dad purchases a VHS video camera, mostly to film my surfs, and I'm able to see what my approach looks like from the outside. When I feel like I've had a subpar session, the video often confirms otherwise. I endure my dad's cornball commentary, as well as him usually missing my best wave, and I study the videos endlessly to see where I can get better. The newspaper article puts a chip on my shoulder; I'm intent on proving that I'm not among the few dozen best in town, but THE best. Or, at least second best, behind OMG Wes.

In California, my parents drop me off at a Motel 6 in Ventura where the other All-Stars are staying. For a few days, I spar with the East Coast's brightest talent, including Kelly Slater. The opportunity to share the lineup with elite surfers, to receive coaching from team captain Bruce Walker and others, and to enjoy consistent waves in the middle of summer is priceless. At only 14 years old, Kelly wins the contest (duh!). I fall out early, but I show I can hold my own with this crew during our freesurfs.

The most lasting memory is of a spoiled West Coast All-Star throwing a tantrum on the beach. He has a tiny, inconsequential ding in his board, which he insists is the reason he loses his heat. Since his mom didn't take him to get it fixed, he berates her in front of everyone. That, to me, encapsulates the difference between the East and West Coast: We're all ridiculously privileged to be able to surf, but at least we aren't as bad as a lot of the Cali kids, raised with waves in the heart of the surf industry. We don't consider it our birthright.

Meanwhile, down the coast, Derrick is competing in a professional event at Malibu. In his signature long-john wetsuit, he advances through several rounds in what will be the apex of his surfing career. After the contest, my parents and sister head back home, leaving my brother, my friend Jeff, and me with our own rental car for two additional weeks. Aside from meals and sleep, we do nothing but surf.

We stay in Huntington Beach for a week with a guy who sponsors us, Gary Ward. Gary owns a company called Trac-Top that makes traction pads for surfboards, and he welcomes us into his home with his wife and baby daughter. For that week, we're part of the family. Toward the week's end, we grow a little jaded after so much surf, and for the first time we decide to skip the windblown afternoon session. Gary isn't hearing it, and he gives us a rousing pep talk to get us back in the water. Decades later, when my oldest son moves to California, Gary rents him a trailer near the beach to live in for several years. He's one of the nicest guys ever.

California surf resembles a good day at home every day, but it hardly inspires awe. Hawaii is a different story, and that same winter we embark on a family trip to the islands. Just as Hatteras is a big jump from 1st Street, Hawaii is like Hatteras on steroids. Oahu is not only the birthplace of modern surfing; every winter, it's the proving ground for the entire sport. Think big waves, big boards, and big Hawaiian dudes who resent pale tourist kids for stealing their island.

We spend a week on the fabled North Shore over Thanksgiving, and there's no better litmus test for how far you want to take your surfing. Derrick and I have a rental car, so we travel wherever the radio surf report indicates is happening each day. We encounter the largest surf I've ever seen, pushing my borrowed 6'1" gun as far as it can go. The last morning, I venture out at the famed big-wave spot Sunset Beach, prompting Derrick to throw in the towel. I realize I'm quite literally in over my head and only catch one wave, but it's enough to squash any lingering semblance of sibling rivalry, at least in terms of surfing.

My parents, to their credit, allow me the freedom to decide on my own what I'm comfortable with. Of course, we exploit their laidback approach by linking up with a couple friends from home for a late-night tour of the underbelly of Waikiki. Somehow, one bar doesn't mind serving alcohol to a 15-year-old. We stay out most of the night, spending the last few hours harassing the prostitutes. Without planning to follow through with any action, we haggle with them for lower prices until the promise of "Sucky-sucky, five dollars" is too much for one of our friends to resist. We have no cell phones to call our parents, so when we finally stumble through the door of our rental condo at 4 a.m., they're understandably pissed. Hawaii expands my horizons exponentially. Any waves on the East Coast suddenly seem like child's play.

While I'm always up for the prospect of going to a party, I don't do much once I get there, at least compared to my classmates. At a typical weekend gathering, I drink a two-liter Bartles & Jaymes wine cooler, usually straight from the bottle. I always head out with high expectations, expecting a scene from *Sixteen Candles* or *Weird Science*. Inevitably, I find myself sitting quietly in a corner. Throughout high school, I smoke weed on a couple of occasions but don't get much out of it and never have the desire to try anything stronger.

Drugs are an escape, and there isn't much I long to escape from. I'm a little socially awkward, but it's nothing a couple liters of fruity wine cooler can't temporarily fix. It's not that I consciously seek to be healthy for surfing—if that were the case, I would work out and pay attention to my diet. I'm just not interested in mind-altering substances, and I'm too cheap to spend much money on anything that won't lead to catching more waves.

My friend Jeff is even more of a teetotaler, so we make a perfect pair. He's a fixture at my house, always happy to help clear some of Mom's leftovers from the fridge. I live right behind First Colonial High School, and we go to my house every day after class to watch surf videos before hitting the beach. Betamax options have expanded slightly, but not much. Our go-to is Quiksilver's *The Performers*, filmed entirely on the North Shore during the winter of 1983–'84. The surf isn't relatable to what we're preparing to ride at 1st Street, but it features OMG Wes and an incredible, bootlegged soundtrack. We wear out the tape and memorize every cheesy word of dialogue.

People in the local surf community refer to me and Jeff as The Dynamic Duo. We spend more time in the water than anyone, regardless of the conditions, and we set our sights far beyond the 1st Street hierarchy. We push one another daily, whether we're surfing or playing basketball, tennis, or some other sport between sessions. The only area we aren't competitive in is with girls, as Jeff is a certified stud, while I get tongue-tied around the opposite sex.

Also unlike Jeff, I'm unable to separate our rivalry from our friendship, at least when it comes to surf contests. I want to win at all costs. Going into the final event of the ESA season for Juniors (15–17), the only way I can catch Jeff in the standings is to win the contest without him advancing to the final. I go so far as to stand behind the judges during his heat, offering commentary about how poorly he's surfing. I win, and don't think twice about how I've achieved it. It's a straight-up Cobra Kai move, except this Johnny Lawrence pulls it on his best friend. Considering I'm so focused on winning that I want Jeff to fail, I'm worse than any '80s movie villain.

Jeff is two years older than me, and at age 18 he graduates high school and turns pro. Without much backing aside from free boards, clothes, and wetsuits, he moves to Carlsbad, California, to be closer to the action. He rents an apartment and gets a job at La Costa Resort doing room service. That allows him to surf all morning, which is always the best time to surf out there. I can't let him have all the fun, so I spend the next two summers camped out on his living-room sofa.

At my graduation, each student is given an index card with their name, and upon reaching the stage, the cards are handed over to be read aloud by the faculty. Those students with honors (3.0 or better) have an asterisk beside their names. My GPA comes in at a 2.97. I use what I remember from rounding numbers back in elementary school math and discreetly draw myself an asterisk. The principal reads my name, with honors, and I walk out of high school for what the last time.

MAY 2014

I've gone four months without surfing, and I haven't tried anything new. I am determined to feel the hole that surfing occupied in my life before deciding how to fill it. The missing-out on riding waves still stings, but Huey has neglected us for a few weeks. I see the ocean from my North End vantage point, and things are different up here. There's no central gathering spot, so I don't run into friends at every surf check. People here are spread over the neighborhood's forty blocks. I long for the camaraderie of going surfing, and I suffer withdrawals from the friendly competition of a surf session. And, with only a few weeks before the return of stifling humidity, I just want to be outside. All of that leads me to one conclusion: golf.

Lots of older folks seem to build their lives around golf the way I have with surfing. Both pursuits are endlessly challenging, fun to do with friends, and full of health benefits. I inherited a set of old hand-me-down clubs from my father-in-law, who happens to be about a foot taller than me. They aren't the perfect set for me, but at least they're left-handed, like me.

I've played a dozen or so rounds in my life, each time

shanking roughly 98 percent of my shots. But that other 2 percent feels so damn good, enough to give me the false confidence that I can capture the magic of those special shots again. Regardless, there's a tournament fundraiser for Wave Warriors Surf Camp, a nonprofit that Ken and I started to treat injured soldiers and their families to a day of saltwater therapy, so I call out sick from work and head to the links.

We drink, gamble (one dollar per hole), joke, and walk around for four hours chasing our balls into the woods and water. Predictably, I hit two shots that feel heroic, and roughly one hundred that frustrate me to no end. I leave the course feeling the same way I did all the other times I've played—filthy, tired, annoyed with my poor play, and muttering, "Oh yeah, that's why I don't golf."

All in all, we have a fun day. Not the golfing, mind you, but the other stuff. After a jaunt to Hatteras, if I've managed to catch even two memorable waves, I leave feeling satiated, happy, at one with nature. Walking off this man-made, meticulously manicured course, I'm pleased that We've raised money for a great cause, yet I cannot escape the notion that 'golf' is just 'flog' spelled backwards. It's torture, self-flagellation, pure and simple.

Typically, if I call out sick for work, it's to go surfing on those rare days when the waves are exceptional. Without fail, so long as I get in the water, I return to school refreshed. Considering the fragile mental health of any middle school teacher, an occasional day to regroup is fully warranted. Either way, it's back to 100-plus hormonal eighth-graders the next day.

My school is in a low-income area that's nowhere near the oceanfront. My students, for the most part, don't know how to swim, much less surf. I have surf posters all over my walls, and I find creative ways to relate surfing to my civics curriculum. With surfing now appearing regularly in commercials, and competitions sometimes aired on TV, I wonder what my kids actually know about it. So, I ask.

Their responses (with authentic spelling preserved) are interesting, to say the least. Most of my students attempt to provide definitions of and parameters for the sport:

- You attempt to ride a wave by gliding against the wave while it makes the circle thing.
- Skate boarding on water without wheels.
- You get a surfboard, go towards the ocean, then catch a wave going back to shore. You can be a 4 year old or even an 80 year old grandpa.
- It's a sport you win by being in the longest distance and longest on the board.
- Can't surf in the sand.
- Some people end up living at the beach because of it.
- I know not a single thing about surfaing except that the object is to ride a wave in the most awesome way possible.

- They put wax on the board to make it smoother.
- Things you need before you surf: a bodysuit, a surfboard, and knoledge on how to surf.
- A board is about three feet long and flat.
- A person gets on a wood board and rides waves.
- There are multiple ways of surfing such as boggy boarding.
- Surfers usually wear a wet suite.
- You get on a bord that looks like a long skate bored and you get on top of it and ride waves.
- The trick of it is to do it while you're on water.
- One surfing move is the hang 10. I know this from the back of a shampoo bottle.

Meanwhile, others offer suggestions for avoiding potential risks:

- Surfing is a sport in which you stand on a board and pull off slick tricks. You musn't do it as a rookie or you could drown.
- Surfing can be very dangerous.
- There are various extensive tricks to learn, and a large amount of safety hazards are present.
- If you are lucky enough you won't get eaten by a shark.
- If you fall you get saved by lifeguards.

Some students wax philosophical or just plain weird:

- When you surf its good to have cleared your mind and to be happy and free your mind.
- Surfing is quiet.
- You need patience because sometimes you can try your hardest but the wave will let you down.
- You don't have to go to college to surf.
- If you are in the middle of the ocean and catch a fish, you should let it go and not put it in your pocket and continue surfing.
- Beyonce likes to do it on her surfboard.
- Surfing is most popular in California or New Mexico because they have better waves than the Atlantic Shore due to gravitational pull coming from the moon.
- Don't wear a shirt or you're lame. And you gotta be tatted so you can look cool.

Clearly, my students' thoughts about surfing are equal parts insightful and ridiculous. Either way, I'm thrilled to see them put legitimate thought into answering a question.

This same month, I spend an evening attending a speaking engagement for school (to earn my required "Professional Learning" points). The speaker is wonderful, so much so that I regret all my bitching beforehand about having to go. He speaks about inspiring children by showing them that we care about their future beyond standardized tests.

The speaker leads with a story about the Greek philosopher Socrates. One day, a traveler asks Socrates how to get to Mount Olympus, and the great thinker replies, "Make sure every step you take is in that direction." The traveler walks off thinking, "No duh, you dipshit!"—but the speaker suggests we share the story with our kids and let them know that we're here to help them reach their Mount Olympus, whatever that may be.

Encouraged by the thoughtful responses to my surfing question, I ask my students to write about their life's goals and what steps they're taking to reach them. Expecting a good fifteen minutes of quiet, I pull out my phone to mindlessly scroll through social media. Before I can sit down, one of my kids pipes up, "Mr. B, what's your Mount Olympus?" There are moments, as a teacher, when you have no answer, and this is one of them. I say, "This is your assignment, not mine," and we both go back to our business.

Or at least the student does. I'm perplexed by the question, and mindlessness is no longer an option. By my age, you should probably have an idea of where you want to be in life. I had dreams, at some point long ago, but who has time for that stuff when there's work to do and kids to raise and waves to ride? As a pro surfer, I've signed posters with the phrase "Never stop dreaming!" But now, I have nothing.

The last goal I can remember is from ten years earlier. I was in Tahiti covering a surf contest for a website I worked for, and Mrs. B flew over to celebrate our tenth wedding anniversary. The only accommodations in the tiny village where the event was being held were with local families, and the only room available was with a crotchety, old lady named Mammy. Mammy lived in a soggy, mosquito-infested house, suffered from elephantiasis, and served fish heads swarming with flies for dinner, so you can see why she might have been a little grumpy. Being in the house made us grumpy, too, but it rained nearly the entire time, so we were stuck.

As soon as the event ended, we hightailed it out of Mammy's and boarded a ferry to Mo'orea, a neighboring island we'd heard was not to be missed. After an hour, we got within sight of Mo'orea and were struck dumb. I'm not sure how much of our vision was tainted by the hellish lodgings of the previous few days, but the island was the most beautiful place we'd ever seen. The lush paradise wasn't too far removed from what Captain Cook and his crew found in these parts hundreds of years earlier. We decided, on the spot, that we'd live here one day, or at least somewhere similarly tropical.

Then, rather than go home and start saving for our future utopia, we sank deeper into debt. We had our third child, continued to neglect budgeting our resources, and were forced to abandon our home for a basement apartment not much nicer than Mammy's house. I expect my 14-year-old students to know what they want out of life, but I'm utterly clueless about my own.

PRO SURFER

The first human to ride waves for fun was likely a Pacific Islander a couple thousand years ago. From then until not long ago, aside from some early Hawaiian gambling, surfing was done exclusively for fun. The first time a surfer earned a living solely from riding waves was around the time I was born, in 1970. Surf magazines began printing in the 1960s, and a hodgepodge professional tour formed in 1976. Photo incentives, prize purses, and monthly retainers steadily grew from there, and in September of 1988, I strap on my leash for my inaugural event as a pro.

I've competed in the Pro Division of the East Coast Surfing Championships (ECSC), the second-longest-running surf contest in the world, as an amateur since I was 14, finishing as high as ninth place. The contest runs in Virginia Beach each August, meaning surfers come from all over to compete in waves they'd never consider riding at home, with most of the competitors struggling to stay afloat, much less muster some kind of forward momentum. In the 1988 ECSC, I remain amateur and win the amateur Men's Division. For the final, I borrow Jeff's webbed gloves made for enhanced paddling. As with acid-wash jeans and popped collars, the gloves are an accepted fashion accessory at the time. I win the final, and, as my fellow high school grads head off to college, I join the ranks of pro surfers.

There's no press conference, no breaking news on SportsCenter, and no screaming groupies. All it takes to become a pro surfer is to enter a contest as a pro, and my debut couldn't be any less conspicuous. In September of that year, seeing there are good waves for an ESA event being held at the VB fishing pier, a few guys decide to throw in some cash for a pro heat. OMG Wes is in town, along with the Floridian Matt Kechele and the usual cast of local rippers. I pay my $25 entry fee, don a Lycra jersey, and officially become a pro surfer.

I win my first heat, advancing straight to the finals. More importantly, I defeat my hero, OMG, and I probably should retire on the spot. I don't, and I go on to finish third in the final, behind OMG and Kechele, respectively. My haul for the event is a whopping $36 (or $11 when you deduct my entry fee). It's quite possible that no other amateur in any sport has ever turned pro for a smaller cash prize.

*****

Thanks to winning the 17th Street/Billabong Surf Series, a group of amateur contests held earlier that year, I earn a ticket to Hawaii and entry into the Billabong Pro, a massive world tour event at Sunset Beach in December.

I promise my parents I'll start school that January, of 1989, which gives me two-and-a-half months to surf my brains out. A bunch of friends from home pool our funds and rent a house along the North Shore.

The world tour comes to Hawaii each winter, along with the staff of every surf magazine, every filmmaker, and every aspiring professional from Victoria to Virginia. Our place is right next to Foodland, the only grocery store around, so surf-star sightings are a daily occurrence. I surf, eat ramen, and sleep, on repeat, the entire time.

For the first few days, it's just me and Harry Fentress, the friend who jumped at the "Sucky-sucky, five dollars" deal a few years earlier. Harry has spent a lot of time here, and proves to be the ultimate tour guide. Tall, loud, and unafraid of confrontation, he shows me the ins and outs of every spot along the North Shore. Somehow, during every session, Harry manages to get into an argument and nearly come to blows with another surfer, before eventually shaking hands and becoming friends. While he's none-to-nose in another screaming match, I'm sneaking past to snatch another wave.

At the end of my third day, I reluctantly follow Harry out to the fabled big-wave spot Waimea Bay. The deadly wave is haunting enough, but when I look up to see the iconic church bell tower and the ancient burial ground perched on the cliff, I'm utterly spooked. Luckily, the waves are harmless, not much above head-high and barely breaking along the rocky point. I get a few easy ones and start to get comfortable, but, as is often the case around here, everything changes in an instant.

I've read stories of surfers being caught in the water in Hawaii during a rising swell, in which conditions flip from fun to fearsome. It's always that someone looks out to sea and suddenly the ocean goes black as a massive wave blocks out the entire horizon. I look out past the rocks a little before dark, and it happens.

I stroke like a madman to get out of harm's way, and just before paddling over it, I hear Harry screaming at me to catch the wave. Turning to face the shore, I execute a few halfhearted paddles. Directly in front of me, the surface is pockmarked with churning boils as the powerful wave sucks water off the rocks below. At the last second, my survival instinct kicks in, and I pull back just in time. Harry, farther inside than me, turns and catches it. I'm left sitting alone in the lineup, my mouth agape. He kicks out way down the line, hooting at the top of his lungs. "Oh my god, why didn't you go?" he froths. "That wave was so good!"

It seems I haven't mastered surfing the North Shore, not even close. In the days that follow, I manage to have my surf trunks ripped off me by a wave at Jocko's, spend three hours bobbing among the crowd at Pipeline for one measly closeout, and watch Harry almost get into a dozen fights. Derrick and a few other friends join us at the house, and the experience of this winter is beyond my wildest imagination. I ride the biggest waves of my life alongside OMG Wes at Waimea, luck into a Christmas session at tiny Pipe with Tom Curren, and attend a free

Devo concert on New Year's Eve at the Hard Rock Cafe in Honolulu.

When it comes time for the Billabong Pro, it turns out I'm not in the event. Rather, I'm the twenty-third alternate, so there's no way I'm getting in. I make quantum leaps in terms of my comfort level in heavy surf, but Sunset Beach still scares the hell out of me, so I'm not too bummed. I'll return to Hawaii several more times, but never for as long or with the same level of commitment. If I'm going to make it in pro surfing, it won't be on the North Shore.

*****

OMG paved the way for Atlantic surfers to attract sponsorship dollars by crashing into the Top 10 in the world during the mid-1980s. I've been getting free boards and clothes for years, but finding financial support proves a challenge. A new East Coast pro tour, the ASP East, has just started, but it's mostly held in Florida. I deliver Chinese food to scrap together enough money to get to most events. Unfortunately, I rarely advance far enough to earn any paychecks. On the rare instances that I make money, it's only a couple hundred dollars. I attend community college, scheduling mostly once-a-week evening classes in order to maximize surf time.

For each event in Florida, OMG commandeers a van from his shop sponsor, and a bunch of guys pack inside for the twelve-hour trip. OMG has recently slipped off the world tour, but he remains among the top competitors on the East Coast. He doesn't want to be away from home and his new wife for a minute longer than he needs to, so we leave the night before the contest and drive straight through, often pulling up to the beach as the first heats hit the water. Once the van starts moving, per OMG's directive, it's not stopping for anything until both tanks run out of gas. If we need to pee, we pee in a bottle. If we need to switch drivers, we do so while traveling with the cruise control set nine miles over the speed limit in the middle of I-95 traffic.

The first time we make the trek with OMG in 1989, there are ten of us crammed into the van. We all assume he's arranged for everyone to stay with his friend Larry Glenn in New Smyrna Beach, but when we pull up to the house, OMG looks at us and says, "This is where I'm staying. I don't know about you guys." He grabs his duffel and heads toward the front door, leaving the rest of us momentarily stunned. It's Florida hot, and there are bugs everywhere, so sleeping in the van will be pure hell. We grab our belongings and scurry along behind him, reaching the front door just as Larry opens it. Luckily, Larry is the nicest guy in the world and welcomes all of us inside.

We repay Larry for his hospitality by inviting the entire beach to a party at his house the next night. He's a single guy, so he goes along with it. We all go out to a local Mexican restaurant, down several pitchers of beer, and pull sombreros and guitars off the walls to entertain the other patrons. When the bill arrives, we throw in some money, but not nearly enough. Larry smiles and covers the difference. By the time we get back to his neighborhood, we have to park way down the street because the party is already raging.

We lose early in the contest, while OMG survives nearly till the end, which will become standard procedure. After a year of this, he begins to falter, and either me or one of the other guys does well. When that's the case, and one of us outlasts him, we return to the beach after our heats to find the van packed and running. Sometimes, he won't wait for the results to be announced, assuring us We've lost and saying, "If we leave right now, we can get to the Georgia Pig by 5 and be home by 2 in the morning. Get in the van!"

While Derrick attends college and works at becoming an artist, he remains my biggest supporter as well as my harshest critic. When I think I'm ripping, he makes a subtle comment such as, "That board looks a little big," and I know what he really means is that my turns look slow. He's the one person who tells me like it is, as painful as it may be to hear. Satisfying sponsors or judges is easy; living up to the standards Derrick sets for me makes me strive for perfection. Without his sincere feedback, I'd never get any better.

When a new surf shop sprouts up in town, Derrick sets about changing my financial situation. He uses his power of persuasion to convince the store's owner, a former sales rep for Ocean Pacific (Op), to flow me a few hundred dollars a month, and the owner hits up Op for a few hundred more. Op's reputation among real surfers isn't good; only tourists still wear their clothes. Money is money, and Tom Curren is an Op guy. I sign their contract as quickly as I can and wait beside my mailbox for the checks to roll in. My brother/agent doesn't ask for a fee; he just wants to see me succeed.

My friend Jeff Hunter gives up on the California pro-surfing dream after two years and returns to Virginia. He hasn't given up on surfing, and we resume our friendship and rivalry. While I no longer lobby the judges for his demise, I'm crushed when he beats me. After he ousts me in the quarterfinals in an ASP East event in Florida, I barely speak to him the whole drive back. Revenge comes as he exits an I-95 rest area with toilet paper hanging from the back of his pants, and I don't tell him until we get home.

*****

Using my influx of sponsor cash, I travel regularly to California to compete on the U.S. tour. While I'm there, I stop by the Op warehouse to handpick some new clothes, which was among my favorite activities when Quiksilver sponsored me over the previous few years. I find the entire Op line hideous and struggle to locate the few garments that don't sport giant neon logos. The only piece I'm excited about is a pair of bright-orange nut-huggers that I'll wear as a joke.

Op sponsors a few young pros, one being Taylor Knox, an upcoming star from Carlsbad. I know Taylor from earlier California visits, and he's a great guy. He'll later become my favorite surfer on tour. But in 1990, Op pays him lots of money compared to me, and they feature him in magazine ads and send him on exotic surf trips for photo shoots. In one of my first Bud Tour events, in Imperial Beach, I advance through a few early heats and come up against Taylor in the fourth round.

To Taylor, it's just another heat on a steady rise toward the world tour. (The U.S. tour is part of a global qualifying tour, whereby the top-ranked competitors at year's end graduate to the World Championship Tour.) To me, this heat is the whole contest. With that mindset, I surf possessed, paddling around guys as though I'm at 1st Street. I finish first, and Taylor comes in second. By the next round, pitted against some random dudes, I lose interest and get eliminated. A few months later, I beat Taylor again in Florida, but run out of gas in the following heat. While I wanted to prove to Op that I deserve the money, exposure, and trips, they instead cut my salary and put me on an incentives-only contract at the end of that year. Luckily, Quiksilver recognizes the need to have a pro in my area and they step up with some money.

I fly solo into LAX for an event in Oceanside. I figure on taking a bus down to the event, but due to a Greyhound strike, I find myself stranded near the airport. An entrepreneurial Mexican guy with a van sees me lugging a boardbag and offers to drive me to Oceanside for $10, so I squeeze in alongside a dozen other passengers, all Mexicans. After a cramped and at times frightening couple of hours, during which we drive through shady areas of Santa Ana and I consider the possibility that my organs are about to be harvested, he drops me at the contest site. Still, I have nowhere to stay and am preparing to sleep in my boardbag under the bleachers. Fortuitously, a guy I sort of know from home, Rich Brown, jogs by with his fiancée just before dark. They offer up their sofa, where I end up crashing for the next week. For another event that year, I plan to stay with my Op team manager, but he has other ideas: as the contest commences, he leaves me and my belongings at the beach and heads home, not to be heard from again.

The next year, I fly to California by myself to do some surfing over spring break, and this time I get the royal treatment. Since I'm only 20, there's only one agency around LAX that will rent me a car, a tiny operation in a shady part of town. On the shuttle ride, I get to talking with a student from Michigan State who is also on a solo spring-break mission. We each get our cars, and before leaving, I ask the attractive girl working the counter if we also get complimentary Lakers tickets. She says, "I used to work for the owner of the Lakers—I'll take you guys to a game." I give Michigan State the number where I'm staying but don't expect a call.

I don't think about it for a few days while I'm off surfing down south, but then I get word from Michigan State that we're to meet Rental Car Girl that day after she gets off work to go to a Lakers game. I arrive as she's getting off, and we all get into her run-down Hyundai and head for the Great Western Forum. We enter the parking area and pull up to the players' lot. The guy working the lot greets her with a warm hello, and we pull in alongside the Bentleys and Rolls-Royces. Michigan State and I look at each other as if to ask, *Is this really happening?*

We stroll into the Forum without tickets and head straight for the Forum Club, Jerry Buss' VIP lounge packed with executives, actors, and groupies. Rental Car Girl has no interest in watching the Lakers play the expansion Minnesota Timberwolves, so she introduces us to Jerry's son Jim, who hands us two tickets for center court a few rows up. I'm a Lakers fan and spend the first half in awe of being so close to Magic and James Worthy, while Michigan State talks about trying to bust a move with Rental Car Girl.

At halftime, we return to the Forum Club to check in, and Jim hands us two passes to the owner's box for the second half. It has a dozen or so seats, and the only vacant spots are right next to 'Bull' (6'8" actor Richard Moll) from the show *Night Court* and his wife. During a timeout, the Laker band launches into the *Night Court* theme song, and the entire arena goes nuts as Bull gets up and starts dancing. We don't spend a penny during the entire experience, but one offhand comment has scored us the night of our lives. Which is the only scoring we do, as Rental Car Girl rebuffs Michigan State's advances.

*****

Over the next few years, I settle into a cycle. In the winter, I get all fired up and drop out of school with dreams of making the world tour. I fly around the country and lose out early in a few events, and then swallow my pride and register for the upcoming semester back in community college. My results along the East Coast steadily improve, just enough to keep my sponsors happy, but beyond that I sustain little success.

Aside from surfing a bunch, I do nothing mentally or physically to prepare for the grind of high-level competition. I haven't worked out since my year as a seventh-grade wrestler. Somebody says that carbo-loading is a good idea, so I shovel down a huge bowl of pasta the night before a contest. My diet is crap. And even though my main job is getting exposure for my sponsors, I avoid photographers if they set up in front of a crowded lineup—if I have to haggle for waves to get shots, I go elsewhere and surf with a few friends.

A big part of my lackadaisical approach is my blind devotion to the Tom Curren mystique. Tom's image is that he just shows up and surfs, not caring for the whole pro circus. I ignore the fact that even Curren, the most naturally gifted surfer of his generation, trains hard. I enjoy being able to do nothing but surf, and it works to an extent. But honestly, I'm only fooling myself.

What it comes down to is this: I strive to surf with excellence, but I'm uninterested in the trappings of being an excellent surfer. Fame bores me, and fortune never drives the pursuit. I experience glimpses of seamless rides, shifting my weight at the perfect times and honoring the distribution of the wave's energy with my own. I want to go fast, because that's the only time I replicate what I felt on my first wave—feeling like I'm flying. I want to make my moves appear easier than they are, because that's what good surfing looks like to me. I want to flow with the wave, let it inform where my board will go and maximize what it allows me to do. Unfortunately, ticking these personal boxes rarely equates to professional success.

One day, I bring some photos to one of my sponsors to use for a potential magazine ad. As we sit there in his massive office, he studies the images and tells me, "These are good, but you need to extend yourself more. You're surfing too compact. You're making it look too easy." In one photo, other than the nose of my board, I'm completely hidden from view inside the tube. He studies the image and says, "We can't use this. We can't see enough of your board here. We can't run an ad if we can't see you. If you were Curren, sure, but you're Borte. Nobody knows who Borte is."

During hurricane season, I head down to Hatteras with OMG Wes and a photographer from *Surfer* named Kevin Welsh. A younger guy from VB, Jason Griffith, is supposed to join us, but he's not answering his phone.

We drive to his house and yank the kid out of bed, not giving him a chance to say no. The waves are perfect, crystal-clear tubes all day. A few weeks later, Welsh says that *Surfer* is considering using a shot of me for the cover, that it's between one other shot and mine.

I happen to be heading out to California for a contest, so Welsh suggests I pop into the *Surfer* offices to say hello and check out the pics. I don't know anyone there, but Welsh has called ahead to set it all up. In a small waiting room, a receptionist asks my name. "I'm Jason Borte—Kevin Welsh sent over some shots of me, maybe a cover shot?" She eyes me dubiously and disappears through a door to corroborate my story. I flip through some mags on the table, wondering how I'll look on the cover. She returns with a smile and says, "Uhh, the editor isn't in right now; maybe you could try back later."

Defeated, I trudge back to my car, imagining everyone having a good laugh inside the office. The next month, the new magazine appears in surf shops around the country. On the cover, it's not me, but my friend Jason Griffith, the kid I woke from a dead sleep to go to Hatteras that day.

Even when I extend myself and try to become a self-promoter, it doesn't work. While I appear in a handful of ads and videos, and I sign plenty of posters at Quiksilver promos, I'm a mere blip in the world of surfing. My goal is to be a pro, and I'm doing it, barely. Extending myself means committing to that dream completely, something I can't bring myself to do. In my mind, failure is too big of a risk.

Jeff at least followed his pro-surfing dream out in Cali before moving home and taking over one of his mom's salons. He's given it his all, and he happily moves into the next phase of his life. But at age 23, he suffers a seizure, never having had any previous health issues. Six months later, it happens again. After a bunch of tests, there's talk of a pacemaker to safeguard against his irregular heartbeat, but nothing is done. Several months later, all seems back to normal.

On the morning of October 24, 1992, I swing by the salon on my way to the beach. Jeff and I make plans for an afternoon session, which turns out to be a lot of fun. I surf the rights near the jetty while he dominates his customary lefts down the beach. After a couple hours, I leave him to get to my job delivering Chinese food. Jeff stays in the water for a while before stopping to visit another friend to check out some surf videos. There, he suffers a third seizure. He's rushed to the hospital, but the medical staff are unable to revive him.

I live close by, but by the time I reach the emergency room, Jeff has passed away. They allow me to spend a few minutes alone with him. I've never seen a dead person, and now I'm staring at my best friend's lifeless body. I put my hand on his shoulder and I'm struck by the cold rigidity. There's so much ahead of us: building families, taking our future kids surfing, reminiscing at cookouts about our glory days. Jeff is so much better of a person than me, rarely judging others and never taking a friend for granted. I struggle to accept the reality of the situation.

For Jeff's funeral, another friend of ours, Jesse Fernandez, writes some heartfelt words that I plan to read. Jesse says he grabbed a pencil the night before, and the whole thing poured onto the paper as if written by some outside force. I stand in front of hundreds of mourners, and as I open my mouth to speak, nothing comes out. I gather myself and try again, but still nothing. The rabbi mercifully takes the paper and shares Jesse's tribute on the importance of friendship.

The following year, I round up a bunch of our friends for a day of surfing in Jeff's honor. We create a new T-shirt to commemorate the event, and the gathering becomes an annual tradition. For the next two decades, "The Jeff" is the one day when we all come together to surf, tell stories, and remember our friend. These events become some of the most memorable days of my life, full of camaraderie and hijinks.

With Jeff gone, instead of competing against my best friend, I surf for him. Not only are his initials drawn on my boards; I feel him with me each time I enter the water. I gain a newfound focus and earn results that have forever eluded me. I spend a lot of time with Jesse, a phenomenal older surfer who competes on the ASP East longboard tour, which takes place at the same events as the shortboarders. Jesse lives on the Outer Banks, and he shapes my boards. More than that, he provides invaluable insights into every facet of surfing, from equipment, to diet, to psychology, to energy, and lots of other important areas I've never bothered to consider. He's the closest thing I'll ever have to a coach, and under Jesse's influence, I become one of the top competitors on the ASP East tour.

Living in Virginia, as with much of the East Coast, we either embrace small waves, fail horribly, or get the hell out. For me, making the most of miniscule conditions becomes my calling card. Doing so requires zero bravery, but more technical skill than riding big surf, sort of like a brilliant short game in golf as opposed to the manliness of a huge driver off the tee. In a lineup devoid of any noticeable swell, one must locate and catch waves that are barely there. Then, manufacturing down-the-line speed without flapping like a lunatic is nothing less than an art form. Finally, there's executing some semblance of a legitimate turn, while socking away enough momentum to ride out of it without sinking. For a time, under piss-poor conditions, few other surfers do it better.

However, by the beginning of 1997, commuting to Florida for events is hardly worth the trouble. When I started, it was me and OMG Wes and Ken and a bunch of other guys. We had fun regardless of the outcome. Nine years later, everyone else has real jobs, so it's just me still clinging to the dream. Two days before the first event that season, I weigh the costs and wonder how high I need to finish to break even. Mrs. B, pregnant with our first child, squelches my indecision with, "Fuck that, just go and win it!"

I book a flight to Florida, and as instructed, I win the contest. More often than not, I find myself in the finals that year. Just before the last event of the season, I do some math and realize that no other competitors can catch me in the ratings. I call the tour director, and he confirms that I am indeed the Association of Surfing Professionals East Coast champion. Sitting at home, I celebrate with all my groupies: Mrs. B and our three-month-old baby, Grady.

I don't know it at the time, but the tour is hemorrhaging money and is a few months from folding, meaning this is basically the end of my pro career. Even more quietly than it began—on the day I netted $11 in an impromptu backyard contest—the ride is over.

JUNE 2014

At the end of the last day of school, all the teachers line up alongside the bus loop as per custom to wave goodbye (or good riddance) to our students. Afterwards, we make a mad dash to the principal's office to officially sign out. Then, we're gone in a cloud of dust, disappearing for months of unadulterated freedom. As a teacher, I feel the same way about that moment as I did when I was a student. Summer, after all, is the reason I chose as a clueless 20-year-old to major in education.

But this year, with the break promising slightly less magic than in the past, I'm not in quite as big of a rush. The change isn't anything drastic, but given my own step back, I take the time to notice students as they pass on their way to the buses. I'm surprised to see that some don't look happy at all; a few are even crying, and I can't help but laugh at such incongruous behavior.

I see a colleague who has also taught one of my especially obnoxious children, a punk who made it his mission to disrupt my instruction whenever possible. I ask, "Did you see so-and-so—he's bawling like a baby?" expecting her to respond with, "Yeah, what a little bitch, huh?" I stop in my tracks when she says, "Yeah, poor baby. For a lot of them, this is the only place they feel loved, or safe. Who knows what they're heading home to?"

The procession of buses takes on new meaning, almost like a Bataan Death March. The walls in my privilege bubble are so thick that I haven't considered that these passengers aren't heading to the beach to live out their summer fantasies. For the next few months, many of these kids won't have the nourishment their growing bodies require or the affection they crave. Hell, some of them won't make it through the day without being abused. The buses pull away with horns honking, and there's nothing I can do to stop them.

I invite all my students to my surf camp over the summer, and have done so for years. I know most of them can't afford the cost, so I say they can pay whatever amount their family can afford, or nothing, a promise I've been making since I arrived at the school in 2010. Only one kid has taken me up on the offer, back in my first year. I took over midyear for an elderly woman who'd apparently been dozing off during class, and the students welcomed me by doing everything in their power to convince me to quit. Coincidentally, this student was the biggest troublemaker of the bunch.

His name was Zack, and he reminded me a little of my seventh-grade self. He was a total smartass, blurting out raunchy comments at inopportune times (as far as classroom management, but perfectly timed in the comedic sense) and contradicting me for the fun of it. I'd understood as a student, however, that there was a line, and I was careful not to cross it. Zack barreled over that line and shrugged at each trip to the principal's office. "I don't care," he insisted, and I believe he meant it. The boy I saw at surf camp was a completely different kid, at least in part because, while he was floating atop a hunk of foam in the ocean, I was his lifeline. He had a great week of surfing and couldn't have been more appreciative.

Each year, several students express interest in learning to surf. They study my camp brochure and ask questions about the biggest wave I've ever caught or whether a shark has ever tried to bite me. The dangers inherent to surfing are greatly exaggerated in the public imagination, as evidenced by the fact that more people are injured cheerleading than riding waves. Still, there's always a fear of the unknown. That, coupled with the difficulty of finding a family member to provide a ride to the beach, means that none of my students make it to camp.

At some point during my mid-30s, having seen enough of the world to realize the luxuries I've been afforded, I began to dabble in giving something back. All I had to offer was the thing I'd so selfishly pursued for so many years—the gift of surfing. Perhaps not coincidentally, my family's favorite show at the time was *My Name Is Earl,* a sitcom about a small-town criminal who discovers karma and goes about righting his extensive list of previous wrongs. I didn't make a list, but I was all about making deposits in my heavily overdrawn karmic bank account.

By 2014, I volunteer at free surf camps for kids with autism and for paraplegics and hold my own camps for foster children and injured soldiers. Wave Warriors Surf Camp (the camp I started for injured servicemen and women) is in its fifth year and has grown to accommodate more than fifty soldiers, as well as their families, for an entire weekend of entertainment and saltwater therapy. Thanks to the vision and efforts of a bunch of great people, the event far exceeds the expectations I had when I rounded up a dozen soldiers and simply took them surfing that first time.

Religion wasn't discussed in my house growing up, but the Golden Rule was repeated often. My parents always tried to help those less fortunate, simply because it's the right thing to do. My dad attended Sunday school as a kid, but only until he got a paper route at age 12 and began running the streets. My mom was raised Jewish, but aside from celebrating the big holidays, the religion didn't have an influence over her life. The only times we stepped into a church or synagogue were for weddings or my cousins' bat mitzvahs.

Going on six months without surfing, my belief in the spiritual viability of riding waves has only deepened. Sure, staying on top of the forecast is frustrating, and trying to find a window of favorable conditions is stressful, and the entire pursuit can be selfish. Every religion has its faults. Still, if I subscribe to any dogma, it's like the pioneering waterman Tom Blake said, "Surfriding is a prayer of a high order...the sea is a beautiful church, the wave a silent sermon." I want to share all of this with my students, to show them not only the beauty of the ocean but also that they can achieve anything they set their minds to. But no matter how many kids show interest during the year, by the time those buses pull away, I won't hear another word from them.

HIGHER LEARNING

In the sixth grade, just before surfing hijacks my every waking thought, my brain remains unclouded. I'm still new to Lynnhaven Middle School and this more upscale area, freshly yanked from my Green Run roots. One day, in Mrs. Wise's English class, I hear, "Mr. Borte, please see me after class," and I figure one of my smartass comments has landed me in hot water. My peers leave, and I drag myself to her desk. "Mr. Borte, we have an awards assembly coming up in a few weeks, and I'd like you to get up and read a poem," Mrs. Wise says.

I'm not in trouble; it's far worse than that. Mrs. Wise sees something in my snappy wit, something like potential. Of her many students, I'm the one singled out. Instead of rewarding me with something cool, she decides on torture, putting me in the most vulnerable position imaginable. I try to decline her generous offer, but Mrs. Wise isn't taking no for an answer. At the assembly, I step onto the stage, open the dusty book to the marked page, and race to the end. The author spouts some nonsense about bringing joy to others, and I clearly don't believe what I'm selling.

Six years later, fresh off the plane from my extended

trip to Hawaii, I'm due to begin classes at Old Dominion University (ODU) in Norfolk. Neither of my parents finished college, but somehow, it's never a question whether my siblings and I will attend. At 18, I have no clue what I want to study, or even if I want to study. I'm going to school, and that's that. The ODU campus is nearby, a forty-minute drive from the beach, and, well, Derrick went here, so it's a given that I'll follow.

On a blustery January morning, I wake early and drive to campus to begin my first 9 a.m. class. I park and walk into what I think is the correct building. It's not. I walk into another, and another, neither of which are the right one. After two months of tropical weather and epic surf, the culture shock is too much for me. Rather than try another building or ask for directions, I find a payphone. "I can't find my class," I tell my mom. "I'm going to community college."

Three years later, after dropping out and coming back, and dropping out and coming back, I'm still at community college. My grades are decent, aside from Introduction to Business, a course I find unbearable. I'm not sure how much blame belongs with my monotoned professor, but I barely attend. By the end of it, I know nothing about business and have my only failing grade. My parents say I need to decide on a major, but nothing sparks my interest. More to the point, I know what I want to do, but majoring in surfing isn't an option.

The day my future will be decided can't be any dreamier. It's one of those spring afternoons when humanity seemingly rediscovers this great place known as the outdoors, but the deadline of a decision refuses to let me enjoy the weightlessness of the idyllic weather. I drive toward home with my left arm protruding out the car window, climbing and dropping against the oncoming air. This, by the way, mimics the feeling of surfing as closely as anything. *Choose a major, ugh.* Nothing comes.

Then, it hits me: *Geez, it's warm, summer-ish even. When I get a real job, summer will cease to exist. I need a career where you don't have to work all year. Wait, teachers get their summers off. That's it, I'm going to be a teacher.*

Just like that, my career path is settled. The only teachers I know are my friend Chip's parents. His dad has become a principal, but his mom remains in the classroom. They are only a few years from retirement. Chip is away at college, but I'm excited to tell his parents and drive straight to their house. Once inside, I share the wonderful news: "I decided I'm going to be a teacher."

His mother lets out an agonizing cry and says, "Oh no, why would you want to do that?" His dad is more to the point: "That's the stupidest thing you could ever do. Don't do it." *Pfft, what do they know?* I declare my major as education and check into transferring back to Old Dominion.

For three years, I attend classes at ODU. And when I say I "attend classes," that's all that I do. I don't spend a moment more than I need to around campus. I don't join a club, don't gather with a study group, don't step foot in a fraternity house, and don't attend a single party. I try to register for once-a-week classes, typically grouped into a couple days and preferably in the evenings. By preserving my days and long weekends, school hardly gets in the way of surfing. I hate wearing a watch, but I wear one to class so I can be sure not to linger any longer than required.

ODU's education department has a good reputation, or so I've been told. Maybe the good professors teach morning classes, leaving the bozos— some of whom have trouble forming a coherent sentence, much less presenting an informative lecture—to handle the weekly evening courses. One woman has a problem with always saying "umm," but it comes across as "ohlm." She says it so often that it becomes all I hear: "Ohlm, the, ohlm, uh, ohlm..."

Most of my education courses focus on a trendy method of teaching literacy called the Whole Language Approach. The premise is to abandon the teaching of phonics in favor of encouraging guessing. Within a few years, it will be tossed aside for the next new teaching theory.

Aside from that, two things stand out from my time at ODU. One is that my aunt Kathy is in one of my math classes, as she's also studying to be a teacher. We get to hang out together for a bit, which is nice. The other is a run-in I have with my creative-writing professor. His class is where I first find enjoyment in writing, so for that I owe him some credit. However, we're supposed to keep a daily journal, which he collects and allegedly reads. I don't believe he reads each entry, so I call his bluff. In order to fill the requisite page, I begin insulting him with lines from *Monty Python and the Holy Grail*, one of my favorite films:

"I unclog my nose in your direction!" "You English bed-wetting type!" "Your mother was a hamster and your father smelt of elderberries!" "You tiny-brained wiper of other peoples' bottoms!"

Turns out, he reads every word. After class, he calls me aside and has me follow him to the dean's office. We sit, and there, on the dean's desk, is my journal. The professor opens the journal to my cheeky comments, reads them aloud, and demands an explanation. Jokes aren't funny when you have to explain them, so my retelling of King Arthur approaching the French-held castle and getting berated by the guards draws nary a smile. I'm threatened with punishment if it happens again, and we all leave.

The professor clearly lacks any sense of humor, as he then has me follow him to his office. We sit down, and he stares at me across his desk. For a long moment, he lets the tension build. Then he asks, "Do you want to hit me—is that why you wrote those things?" I laugh, and he says, "I don't find it funny." Again, I explain that I didn't think he read the journals and assumed that, if he did, he'd pick up on the joke. Instead, he leans back in his chair and crosses one leg over the other, making a point of showing off his well-worn cowboy boots. "If you want to fight, I'll fight you," he says. "I like to fight." I'm angry that he's wasted an hour of my time, but I assure him it won't happen again, and that's the end of it.

I survive the class, and seven years after being lost and bailing to community college, I earn my bachelor's degree, this time with actual honors. As much as I dislike going to school, it's a better alternative for me than getting a job. So, I stick around at ODU long enough to also earn a master's degree in education.

JULY 2014

Boredom is good. The experts agree that tedium leads to contemplation, creativity and problem-solving. Since most humans carry a tiny computer in their pockets, or more often in their hands, nobody has an opportunity to get bored anymore. Smartphone or not, July—an entire month without work or surfing—promises to test my limits of boredom. And since I've found nothing with which to replace riding waves in my life, it's time to get creative.

Historically, July is the flattest month in Virginia Beach, when water temps push 80° and offshore winds lead to more waves heading out to sea than coming toward shore. One week in, that notion is turned on its head as hurricane season gets an early start with a storm named Arthur. While the track is too close to the coast to make good waves, Arthur nonetheless creates plenty of action. Head-high doesn't usually happen here in July, so every surfer within striking distance is on it.

The water is too inviting to miss, so I swim into the lineup and just...bob. I tread water in the impact zone and play cat-and-mouse with the exploding lips, which proves not just a great workout but also heaps of fun. Hurricane fever has infected the surfers around me, raising their expectations to impossible levels that only lead to disappointment. While they curse each closeout, I wash up to the beach an hour later completely happy.

Two weeks later, I drive to Rhode Island, as I do each summer, to hold a surf camp at a little beach town called Weekapaug. Just as I hadn't thought of "bob" as an action verb, the same goes for "summer." While wintertime in Weekapaug is reserved for snowdrifts and tumbleweeds, it's a favorite spot to summer for wealthy folks from all over the Northeast. For years, I've visited the town, each time repeating a cycle of tennis on fake grass, getting kicked off the go-kart track for my aggressive driving, a round of pitch-and-putt (far more enjoyable and less time-consuming than real golf), reading by the pool, sipping mixed drinks, eating fresh seafood, and surfing. By facing south rather than east, Rhode Island's coast receives ample summertime surf.

I'm thankful to have so many distractions for the week, but when the weather turns ugly and the surf really comes up, all the other outside options become moot. After more than 200 days without surfing, I consider the fact that I am 400 miles from home and could easily score a session without anyone knowing. I'm staying with a family of surfers, including three of my camp instructors, and they all laugh at my ridiculous project as they head out the door to surf.

If I only had a GoPro, I lament aloud, thinking I could make myself useful. They have one, of course. I taught the entire family to surf the first year I summered there, and They've all become avid waterpeople, even the mom. After they give me a brief tutorial, I waddle into the shorebreak to try my hand at surf photography.

For two hours, I tread water and snap photos. All the boys get lots of waves, but I doubt they have more fun than me. Summering, it turns out, does not necessarily require surfing.

I'm reading a memoir called *Turtle Feet*, about a piano prodigy who quit Berklee College of Music to become a monk in India. The author, Nikolai Grozni, notes that "despite having free will, people were often incapable of altering the course of their lives or even straying from a purely circumstantial narrative." Grozni laments our penchant for sticking with prefabricated narratives, claiming, "I didn't have to be the person everyone expected me to be."

Any other year, Grozni's sentiments wouldn't have caught my attention, but this isn't any other year. I've clung to what seemed like a prefabricated narrative for most of my life. And while I hardly live a monk's existence, I feel like I'm on a similar path. The book's final line really strikes a chord: "In order to understand something clearly, one must first give it up." I've spent the year asking myself, "Why am I not surfing?" But the question really should be, "Why *was* I surfing?"

I like to believe that what impels me is that it's so much fun. Anyone who's ridden a wave will confirm that there's no more pleasurable pastime anywhere. Still, I can't deny paddling out on occasion with an unconscious desire to escape feelings of inadequacy. On land, I get the sense that I'm not good enough. The ocean, as cheesy as it sounds, washes away my awkwardness. It's a wild environment, yet I understand it. I can't control it, but I know my place in it. With every stroke back out to the lineup for another wave, I'm also stroking my ego.

WRITE STUFF

For most pro surfers, when it's over, it's completely over. A guy I know from Florida went all out to qualify for the world tour one year. At the start of 1991, he took out loans, trained his ass off, and put everything he had into professional surfing. Unfortunately for him, the talent wasn't there. He barely cracked the Top 100, nowhere near the cutoff, and I never saw him again. He didn't quit surfing; people don't do that. He worked to pay off his loans, went to school, and began a career in something or another. There's no way I can do that, too.

Seeing the direction this guy's life went, I never fully commit to pro surfing for fear of a similar fate. Instead, I half-ass my way through school and surfing until I reach a crossroads. 1997 is the best year of my life: I earn a master's degree, win the East Coast pro tour, and become a father. Then, all of a sudden, the tour vanishes, and I have to support my son's expensive habits of eating and soiling his diapers. The following year, I do the unthinkable, taking a job teaching sixth grade at an area middle school.

I learn to tie a necktie, and the principal expects me to be present inside the building when the bell rings each morning. Aside from these inconveniences, I enjoy teaching. My school is a few blocks from the beach, and I skip out during my planning block to go surfing. Still, the job is not covering my bills. We've purchased a lot in a quaint neighborhood a few blocks from the beach, but we don't have the money to build a house. In fact, I get a "for sale" sign and prepare to unload the lot.

Meanwhile, a massive industry has grown around surfing, and business is booming. Had I been born much earlier, that wouldn't have been true. Surfers of yesteryear had actual jobs and went to the beach on their time off. Through the '60s and '70s, careers sprouted up around boardbuilding, magazines, apparel companies, and shops to deliver the sport to the masses.

My friend Jeff's death was the biggest tragedy I've experienced, but it inadvertently leads me toward a new career. When Jeff passed in 1992, the editor of *Surfer*, Steve Hawk, asked me to write a short piece about Jeff's life. Each year thereafter, I write about "The Jeff," the small annual gathering of Jeff's friends, for an East Coast magazine called *Eastern Surf*. After graduating, I send these articles to *Surfer* and *Surfing* magazines in hopes of landing a job.

It takes six months for Steve Hawk, *Surfer's* editor, to sift through his stack of mail and read my letter. By then, it just so happens they're looking to fill a position for East Coast Editor. Steve believes my surfing lends credibility to my writing, which could improve under his tutelage. He flies me to Orange County so I can visit the *Surfer* offices and get to know everyone. As we walk into the building from lunch one afternoon, Steve spots a skateboard poster someone has left on a table. He stops and says, "Hey, that's Tony," and keeps walking. I look down at the poster, and it clicks that Steve is Tony Hawk's big brother—talk about credibility! And I nearly crap myself a few days later, as I'm captioning some photos at Steve's desk, when Tony pops through the door asking if I know where Steve is. That's what it's like at the magazine—you never knew which legend will drop by next.

The magazine work is part-time, so I still need the teaching gig. I enjoy writing, and my travel expenses are covered wherever I go. I begin chasing storms up and down the East Coast and turning those surf missions into articles, finding that the Atlantic has a wide variety of lineups. In every state along the East Coast that I visit, the setups are better than in Virginia. It blows my mind that these places have quality pointbreaks with mellow crowds, illustrating the silliness of my stomping grounds of 1st Street.

Hawk proves a good teacher, offering suggestions rather than taking what I write and fixing it himself. I've had no training in journalism, and no training in writing other than assignments from my angry creative-writing professor. Hawk orders rewrites and makes me consider, for the first time, how to craft an article rather than merely writing whatever comes to mind. Above all, he instructs, "Seek first to entertain, then to inform." Hawk lets me stay at his house when I go to California, and seeing how he interacts with his young son, lying on the floor and having a battle with *Star Wars* figures, I realize what sort of dad I want to be.

For years, I pore over the words of my favorite surf writers—Dave Parmenter, Derek Hynd, and Matt Warshaw—reading and rereading their articles. Surf-travel stories are among the most boring collections of words ever written—*We journeyed a long way, the waves sucked, then it got epic*—but Parmenter changes everything. His dry humor and melodic wordsmithing make his travelogs magical. Hynd's specialty is breaking down the world tour, and his scathing Top 44 previews have me tearing through mags to find them. Warshaw is the keeper of surfing's history, and his profiles reset the bar. Suddenly, I find myself sitting in editorial conferences alongside these guys and others. I hardly feel worthy of breathing the same air, much less using it to share my thoughts. Luckily, the meeting always revolves around surfing, allowing me to show that I'm not a complete kook.

Surfer expands my role, sending me on interesting assignments in Barbados, Portugal, and Cuba. The latter is especially eye-opening, as few people have surfed around "the forbidden island" at that time. We experience the rustic beauty of Havana, pioneer unridden waves, eat horse burgers, and manage to get chased by Castro's machine-gun-toting soldiers. The highlight is meeting a kid who shapes his own boards out of the foam from inside a refrigerator door using a potato peeler. That experience provides a great opportunity as a writer, and an even better one as a human.

When the dot-com explosion reaches surfing in 1999, Hawk is poached to assemble an editorial team for Swell.com. The site meshes newfangled surf cams with extensive daily content, aiming to profit from the expected demise of surf shops in favor of online shopping. Millions of dollars pour into the site, allowing them to pay top dollar for an all-star team of writers and photographers. Hawk sends me a list of available positions, and tells me to pick what I want to do. I like the idea of working from home, in my boxer shorts, so I skip any role that requires me to show up in the West Coast office. We settle on Archival/East Coast Editor, along with assignments covering world-tour events around the globe. I'll get to do what I want, while also allowing my wife and I to afford our lot and build a house.

Then, I recall, I already have a job. The day before Christmas break, I visit my principal and give him the news that I'm quitting. He's not thrilled, but I tell him I'll stick it out until the end of the semester, which is one more month, to give him time to find a replacement.

My main project at the site is "Surfing A-Z," an online encyclopedia of the most important people, places, and events in our sport. To get started, I craft a list of a few hundred entries that I plan to include. My typical day consists of choosing a couple entries that interest me, gathering some background, and writing. Of course, I also have the flexibility to play with my kids and go surfing whenever I want.

While working for *Surfer* put me in close contact with my writing heroes, "Surfing A-Z" has me on the phone with all the legends of the sport. I speak with nearly every major player in surfing, including Tom Curren. It only takes an hour of staring at my phone before I can go through with dialing his number, but after stammering through a few questions, I settle down.

At the time, Curren has long since retired from pro surfing, as has Kelly Slater, who won six world titles and is taking a few years away from competition to refocus. Slater is already considered the greatest surfer ever, but he's keeping a low profile (as low as one can keep while dating Pamela Anderson).

Meanwhile, the biggest name in the sport is the Hawaiian Laird Hamilton, who is then leading the revolution toward big-wave tow-in surfing. Laird is a massive human, and he has just ridden the heaviest wave anyone has ever seen, a cartoonish monster at Teahupoo, Tahiti. I've never spoken to Laird, so I don't know him aside from what I've seen in surf videos or in his role as the narcissistic pro Lance Burkhart in the Hollywood movie *North Shore*. He seems like the same dude in both instances, so for his "Surfing A-Z" entry, I write that he basically plays himself in the film.

One day, I walk into my office to a voicemail from Laird Hamiton. "This is Laird," he says in his typical, booming tone, "I guess you know why I'm calling. Call me back, immediately!" *Holy shit,* I think, *what have I done?* My smartass comments have gotten me in trouble again. Knowing there is 5,000 miles between us, I reluctantly dial his number. Turns out, I've written an article for Swell.com explaining a brouhaha over some photos of his historic wave, and he's calling to offer his input. I breathe a huge sigh of relief that he doesn't want to kill me after all. Nevertheless, I quickly go in and change his A-Z entry to reflect what a nice guy he is.

In addition to the "Surfing A-Z," Swell sends me to cover world-tour events in South Africa, Fiji, Tahiti, France, and Hawaii. On some of the journeys, I figure out a way to bring my family. The window for these contests is two weeks, but they only need around four days to complete an event. Whenever the contest isn't running, I'm paid to hang out with the best surfers on Earth at the best surf spots on Earth.

Inevitably, the old 1st Street competitive spirit rears its head, and in freesurfs around the tour guys, I do my best to keep pace. I'm 30, older than most anyone on tour, yet I more than hold my own. I interview one competitor after a heat, the Californian Keith Malloy, whom I happen to have recently beaten at ECSC earlier that year. Keith turns the questions around and asks, "How does it feel to be covering events where you surf as good as half the guys on tour?" I can't decide if he's complimenting or insulting me. Either way, I love my job.

Surfers everywhere click onto our site, which earns a Webby Award for best sports site in 2001. There's one problem: People aren't ready for an online surf shop. We burn through tens of millions of dollars in investment capital, and there's hardly any cash coming in. In reality, the dot-com bubble burst before our site even went live. Amazingly, we manage to keep much of the team intact for a couple years. But, by 2002, the end is imminent. They've already let go most of the staff.

One night I'm reading to Grady before bed when I get a call from Sean Collins, the site's owner and the man who took surf forecasting to the Internet. He says I'm being laid off. We chat for a bit, and he comments that he can't believe how well I'm taking the news. Some other guys must have cried or called him names, but when he explains I'll be receiving a month of severance pay, the whole thing sounds pretty good to me.

I shrug and go back to Grady and our book. The notion of worrying doesn't enter my mind. I have a big house payment and, by then, yet another mouth to feed, but I have a whole month to figure it out. And, as I've discovered, things have a way of working out for me.

Derrick suggests I file for unemployment. I gather the forms but can't bring myself to fill them out. It doesn't seem right, like I don't deserve it because I haven't really worked in the first place. Asking the government for money is something you do as a last resort, when you have nowhere else to turn. I'm not even close to that point.

A few months earlier, I noticed that Tony Hawk had released an autobiography, and I reached out to Kelly Slater to see if he was interested in doing something similar. He said he had too much going on to think about it at the time—but then, right around the time my severance dries up, I get an email from Kelly saying, "Hey, remember that book you mentioned? Let's do it."

The same publisher that printed Tony's autobiography, a subsidiary of HarperCollins called ReganBooks, has approached Kelly. They just need a writer. Apparently, Kelly tries to enlist Steve Hawk, but they decide that someone closer to Kelly's age and background makes more sense. Steve recommends me, and Kelly puts me in touch with his manager to work out the details.

The manager is a fast-talking New Yorker who seems set on getting Kelly away from surfing and into Hollywood. He sends over a paltry contract, one with zero royalties or travel expenses, and I'm hesitant. The manager calls me and barks, "Look, your writing isn't what's gonna sell this book, okay? Kelly's eyes on the cover are going to sell this thing to 12-year-old girls. We have three other guys in line behind you, so take it or leave it!" The guy is not well-liked in surfing circles, and I understand why. He's all about the bottom line, but I guess that's show business. I go over the manager's head straight to Kelly, who quickly agrees to my requests.

The truth is, I'd have written the book for free. It's an incredible opportunity, and, well, I don't exactly have much going on at the time. I dive right into it, building a list of questions. Having witnessed Kelly's rise from early on, I'm familiar with his story, but I'll need much more. I reach out to everyone I can think of who is close with him, adding their stories to my list. Then, I enlist the help of Matt Warshaw, who is busily constructing *The Encyclo-*

pedia of Surfing from his home in San Francisco. Warshaw mails me a packet of every article written about Kelly, including a wonderful profile that Warshaw penned for *Surfer* a couple years earlier.

I fly to Oahu for a couple weeks at the outset of winter to begin working with Kelly. Like every year, retired or not, he is wintering on the North Shore, where he'll be competing in the Pipe Masters. He's already won the event a record five times, and I arrive as the waiting period begins. Most days, we meet at the Johnson house overlooking Pipe, where we can keep an eye on the lineup. Jack Johnson, a former pro surfer and longtime friend of Kelly's, has recently released his first album, *Brushfire Fairytales,* on his way to musical stardom.

Each day, Kelly and I spend hours discussing the events of his life, methodically exploring each topic on my list. His dad, Steve, who is undergoing treatment for cancer, is also in town to watch the contest. Amazingly, it's the first time in his son's illustrious career that he's attended a world-tour event. Steve is so moved watching Kelly compete that he's in tears. For Kelly, witnessing his father's failing health makes him aware of his own mortality, opening him up to discussing his life for the book.

What awes me most about Kelly isn't that he recalls nearly every heat of every contest in great detail, although that's pretty impressive; rather, it's how he responds to the endless procession of strangers who recognize him along the North Shore. Whether they ask for a photo, some free Quiksilver gear, or the chance to blather about having witnessed one of his many accomplishments, Kelly gives each of them a few moments and a smile. He doesn't take his position for granted, displaying patience for the many people who, ultimately, subsidize his lifestyle.

On my final afternoon, after a close runner-up finish at Pipe, we sit in Jack's backyard and discuss Kelly's future. He plans to return to the tour the following year at age 30, hoping to add a seventh world title to his mantel. He stares out at the sea and notices a 10-year-old Q-tip named John John Florence walk past carrying a board on his way to the surf. The youngster is already well known in the surfing community as a future star, and Kelly says he hopes to one day compete against John John at Pipe. The comment seems laughable, considering Kelly will be in his 40s by the time the kid is on tour, but I can't tell if he's joking.

I fly home and barricade myself in my office for the winter, trying to replicate Kelly's voice in telling his story. At the end of it, I go to Florida and dig through his condo closets for photos, laying out where I want each to go. The publisher takes my advice for the cover, which features a surf shot rather than highlighting Kelly's majestic green eyes. The book, *Pipe Dreams,* peaks at number twenty-nine on the New York Times Best Seller list for hardcover nonfiction.

As a gift, Kelly offers me a custom board from Channel Islands, one of his sponsors and the world's most popular board brand at the time. Rather than take it for myself, I want to show my appreciation to Steve Hawk for all he's done for me. I call Steve and tell him he can order whatever board he wants. He has a big surf trip to Fiji coming up, and hearing his genuine excitement gives me more satisfaction than any board ever could have.

I stay busy with freelance jobs for a while, and then I get another call from Steve. *Surfer* has asked him to find a new editor, and he thinks I'm the man for the job. A decade after they wouldn't let me inside the office—when I couldn't so much as speak to an editor—they're asking me to run the magazine. The prospect of becoming the editor is the biggest honor I've ever received. Taking the position means relocating nearly 3,000 miles to the West Coast, so it's a major decision. My entire family is in Virginia Beach, and my in-laws have moved here to be closer to their grandchildren. I have established a successful surf camp in town, and all my friends live here. I'm torn.

For a few days, I waffle. There's so much about the move that would upgrade my life—the waves, the weather, the opportunity to be at the pinnacle of my profession. If Steve believes in me, I know I can do a good job. Still, somewhere inside, there's a fear of failure. *Surfer* is my bible, has been since I was a kid. And there's something to be said for roots and family and all that sentimental stuff. I decide not to pursue the job, opting to stay in Virginia Beach over Southern California. I struggle to understand why I'm so devoted to a place that causes me such frustration. Am I crazy, or just plain stupid?

AUGUST 2014

August signifies so many things in Virginia Beach. After We've spent months groveling to extract any bit of juice from a wave, hurricane season heats up. We snap out of the summer doldrums with surf that packs the power to knock you on your ass. I don't know if other surfers on the East Coast feel the same way, but I relish a good wipeout and underwater thrashing as a reminder of our place in the world. On land, man can feel like a conqueror, paving over nature and imposing our will on the environment. The ocean doesn't stand for that crap, and it reminds us, in a good way, of how small and insignificant we really are.

And it means ECSC—the East Coast Surfing Championships.

As a competitive surfer in this place, there's nothing that comes close to the week the ECSC comes to town. It's the end of summer, the final week of freedom before my forced march off the sand and into the classroom. It's our—the locals—annual shot at greatness, our chance to prove to the surfing world that no one can come into our house and push us around. Most guys who are successful all over the world rock up to 1st Street and are rendered powerless by the gutless surf. I quit traveling for competition in my early 30s, but I kept doing the pro division of ECSC into my 40s. I refused to join the old men in the amateur age brackets, but as long as I wasn't embarrassing myself versus the pros, I kept entering. My goal each year was the same: send a few visiting hotshots packing, having to return home and say they lost to some gray-haired geezer. Of course, in the end, an out-of-towner always won.

But it's 2014. I'm no longer a competitive surfer, or, for that matter, a surfer at all. I don't even bother to show up at the event anymore, seeing no reason to subject myself to the traffic and the crowds and the mayhem just to watch a few of my friends get beaten by some hotshot visitor in knee-high slop. Competition, under these conditions, is a farce. The event is livestreamed, so I check in at the end of each day to see how the local guys have fared.

I could never have guessed that, when the final hooter sounds on Sunday afternoon, I'll be crying over a surf contest. I've witnessed hundreds of surf competitions since that day back in 1982 when my aunt Kathy and I stumbled upon one at 1st Street. I've seen everything from local amateur gatherings to the largest pro events at Huntington Beach and Pipeline. I've watched careers begin and end, world titles won and lost. I've been thrilled many times, pissed off even more, and bored more than I'd like to admit. But I've never had a tear well up in the process of viewing amped-up dudes in colored singlets attempt to outperform one another while riding waves.

That being said, I'll soon find there is an occasion when it is justifiable to cry at a surf contest, and I'll explain what that moment is.

When you once saw a spindly 6-year-old learning to surf at 1st Street with his dad, getting pushed into whitewater as you rode past into the shorebreak, and you squatted down to his level and shouted, "Yeah, go grom!"

When that kid was 14, and he came to your Sunday-morning coaching sessions, and you gave him a few tips but couldn't tell him the one thing holding him back—that he just needs a few years to fill out.

When the kid was 18 and started traveling all over creation and embedded himself with good surfers and immersed himself in good waves and slogged his way through the trials and tribulations of international competition, a multiyear process, during which he may as well have been in witness protection because he was buried so deep in the ranks.

When he was 20 and you watched random events online, in which the kid was surfing crazy-fast but was still scrawny and unconfident—not unconfident in his ability, but unconfident in whether it was okay for him to knock off the best surfers in the world, even though he was surfing better than them.

When he is now 24 and you tune in to events from around the world and learn that this year is different because the scrawny kid is filling out and gets pissed when he loses to the best surfers, because he should be beating them, and he knows it.

When the kid comes home to the event that hasn't been won by a local guy from 1st Street since OMG Wes took it in 1981, the year before you started surfing, and now you've surfed this event countless times, made the finals a handful of times, once even come in and were told you won and chaired up the beach on the shoulders of none other than OMG Wes, but you ended up in second and had to watch another guy from Florida or California or Brazil or New Jersey somehow finish on top, and you feel like you let all the boys down and you lament that a local surfer might never break through.

When you ignore your hatred of circus atmospheres and pedal your bike through the madness to watch the kid's first heat, and you track him down before he paddles out to assure him, *You got this.*

When you catch bits of his other heats online, heats in which he's crazy-fast, but also cool, radical, powerful, and dominant.

When he hints at this year being different by knocking out last year's champ on the way to the final.

When he's doing well but still losing that final in the waning minutes, destined to fall just short and cause you to kick yourself for wasting time glued to a shoddy webcast showing uninspiring surf when you could've been outside playing with your own kids.

When he doesn't start punching his board in frustration, as you've seen him do many times before, instead remaining focused and utilizing his local knowledge to select that rare 1st Street wave that grabs the sandbar at just the right spot to push back with enough force to allow him to lay into three vicious turns, each of them hacking through decades of pent-up frustration from the local crew.

When the final horn blows and the kid who is no longer a kid enjoys a victory lap with his arms raised clear through the clouds.

When his friends scream from the beach with something they haven't been able to scream with before, something like pride, and they don't wait for him to hit the sand, but rush into the water and hoist him onto their shoulders.

When the 1981 champ, OMG Wes, carries the kid's board behind them, and the entire procession shoots stoke from their pores like fireworks all the way up to the stage.

When you've watched this same parade countless times, but always honoring some surfer from another town or another coast or another country, and you felt none of the emotion, but in this moment, it comes straight out of your screen and into your veins and causes the skin on your arms to erupt into little bumps and the hairs to stand at attention.

When the cameraperson zooms in on the kid's face, and it's the same face that beamed up at you from the whitewater so many years ago at the very same spot.

When you see all that, your vision suddenly goes a little blurry, and it's not because your Internet connection is failing or because your eyes are starting to fail you—although they are. Tears aren't running down your cheeks, not like when you watch the college-football tear-jerker *Rudy*, but you know that you had something to do with what is unfolding, just a tiny bit, because that kid once looked at you and said, *It can be done*. And he went out and did it. And while you haven't ridden a wave in almost nine months, you're as stoked as at any moment in your life.

And when all of that happens, you do something you haven't done in ages: you go down to a bar on the resort strip at almost midnight, even though you have to start school early the next morning, and you walk inside and see a mass of people toward the back. It isn't the normal mass of post-ECSC people, downing drinks to try to forget that some out-of-towner swooped in and looted the top prize. This mass of people is part of you.

You make your way into the middle because the kid is in there somewhere. You find him, and he's still coherent. And when he sees you, his eyes light up. He's honored that you made this effort; you're honored that he's honored. You lean in and all you have to say is, *You're the man.* And you step back to let everyone else tell him. And you sneak out of that bar with your faith restored because it only took you thirty years to discover that everything you do matters, and that surf competition is capable of producing moments of beauty.

BEHIND THE CURTAIN

You know that moment when Dorothy reaches Oz, and she's overcome every bump along the Yellow Brick Road, and she's earned an audience with the great and powerful Wizard, yet he makes her and her friends feel foolish and tells them to beat it, but Toto sniffs him out and pulls back the curtain to reveal not some omnipotent sorcerer but just a feeble, old man pushing buttons to create illusions? Yeah, that's a lot like the surf industry.

As a grom religiously studying surf magazines, I believe in it all: the casual lifestyle that revolves around the oceans' moods, the travel to exotic locations, the fierce competition between the most skilled waveriders in the world, and the brands that package all those dreams for consumption. It's difficult, especially for a youngster, to separate the objective reality of the lifestyle, travel, and contests from the fiction the companies create to profit from said reality.

I am lucky enough, from an early age, to form mutually beneficial relationships with surf companies, allowing me to continue living the dream without having to pay for it with anything other than my soul. After getting into the game with some bit industry players, I link up with the biggest of them all, Quiksilver, at age 16. They hold an event in Hatteras in 1986 called the Warpaint Grand Prix, and my third-place finish against some heavy competition is enough to earn me a spot on their prestigious surf team. A few months later, the company, which was birthed in an Australian garage in 1969 by Alan Green, has its initial public offering.

For the remainder of my teenage years, Quiksilver provides me with clothes in exchange for me slapping their iconic mountain-and-wave sticker on the nose of my board. Being a member of any surf team is a badge of honor, but sporting the Quiksilver logo denotes elite status. Their surf trunks and T-shirts aren't necessarily any better than anyone else's, but when guys like OMG Wes Laine and the world champion Tom Carroll—and later, Kelly Slater—sport that same sticker on the nose of their boards, Quiksilver is the coolest. At one point, the company issues team "credit cards" emblazoned with each rider's name. The card holds no monetary value, but having one's name alongside that logo means instant credibility. OMG Wes once whipped his Quiksilver Team card out at a gas station on the way to Florida, and the attendant tried running it before OMG Wes realized he might be committing fraud and handed the guy a real credit card.

I often hear of someone claiming to be a former pro surfer, as anyone who's surfed in a pro event can technically claim that status—it doesn't matter whether or not they earned a single dime. Aside from a few meager contest checks and some photo incentives, it's really my brief foray with Op in 1990 gets the money flowing in. After that, Quiksilver steps up to a retainer that peaks at $600 per month, in addition to an incentive system for magazine photos and contest results. Bolstered by several smaller checks for endorsing sunglasses, surf accessories, pizza joints, and car dealerships, I bring in enough to cover my bills and some travel.

For me, it's all about figuring out how to get by without a real job. In my mid-20s, like many pros on the back side of a semi-successful career, I straddle the fence and start to inch toward the other side, becoming a "promotions" dude. This means that, in addition to representing Quiksilver myself, I take on the responsibility of passing out stickers and clothes to influential young surfers. I don't realize it, but I've crossed a threshold into the seedy underbelly of the sport. If riding waves or writing about the act is already a suspect means of earning a living, promoting the notion that a billion-dollar company is "grassroots" is straight up snake-oil salesmanship.

Breaking into the surf industry is next to impossible unless you have connections. Being a pro surfer with a decent head attached to my shoulders means I'm welcomed to the party. My retainer gets doubled with my new position, but I realize it isn't nearly enough as soon as I face my first task, cutting the by-then bloated surf team in half. I am in charge of the East Coast north of Florida. The list in front of me has twenty names, all of whom are good surfers, but not all Quiksilver worthy. I highlight for retention the guys who are getting exposure or seem to be the best in their town, and then tentatively began dialing the numbers of those on the chopping block.

No sooner have I broken the news to the first victim before he wails in my ear, certain I've made a mistake. He assures me that he's been ripping at his (very remote) home break and is winning local events in his age bracket. Fair enough, but budget cuts are budget cuts, and I'm just doing my job. I listen with a sympathetic ear for as long as I can, and then wish his whimpering ass good luck and proceed with the next name on the list. That evening, I receive a call from the first boy's father, who's just gotten home from work and been handed the devastating news. "But he's been ripping at our (very remote) home break, and winning local events," the man assures me. And if that isn't enough, the kid's mom calls me later that night, waking me from my sleep with paeans to her son's otherworldly talents. Afterwards, I lay in bed, wondering what the hell kind of trap I've gotten myself into.

Aside from fielding all wishful stories of how hard such-and-such rips at his local beach, my job is to promote the Quiksilver brand. In other words, I'm tasked with selling the company's story, sharing their humble beginnings back in Alan Green's garage and how, despite their Amazon-esque headquarters in Orange County, and their expansion into every shopping mall on the planet, and their newfound billion-dollar status thanks to the rise of Roxy, Quiksilver remains faithful to its hardcore roots. In more mainstream terms, it's like going out and spreading the word that McDonald's is this hip, little burger stand owned by two enterprising brothers.

I make runs up and down the coast to pop my head into surf shops that carry Quiksilver gear and dole out stickers and posters for their customers. Some shop owners are wonderful, guys like Tony G in New Jersey and Kelly Richards in South Carolina, who still surf as much as when they were groms. They got into the business because they loved the sport and wanted to build a life around it. But in many cases, shop owners are kooks who've bought their way into captive audiences for their bullshit surf stories. At 1st Street, I learned that a loud-mouthed kook is a loud-mouthed kook, no matter what you do on land. I force a smile and remind myself that this is still better than a real job.

Quiksilver still expects me to be an ambassador for the brand as a surfer, but doing so leads to further conflicts. As the team manager, I'm supposed to promote my athletes and help them improve. Apparently, that doesn't mean schooling the teamriders in contests. I compete in ECSC throughout my 30s and occasionally come up against my sponsored guys. When I make the finals for the last time at age 35, I'm scolded for having dispatched some visiting Quiksilver riders.

The funnest part of my job is joining Matt Kechele, my Quiksilver counterpart for Florida and the Gulf Coast, to conduct summer surf-camp tours. I worked at a camp in Virginia Beach for a couple summers and find that teaching kids to surf brings me back to when I learned myself. Plus, Kechele, once you get past his rigid exterior, is the world's oldest grom, always either surfing or Huckleberry Finn-ing his way into an adventure. I once watch him, in his 40s, surf for eight straight hours in Costa Rica, right through both high and low tide. Another time, he spent four nights hunting giant "banana" rats in Guantanamo Bay, finally nabbing a monster at around 1 a.m. on the final night of the trip.

Another worthwhile project is creating a short video with Slater and Tony Hawk on the importance of school. Each of these guys attended high school while earning more money than their teachers. When I interview them, they reminisce about the benefits of learning in a classroom with other students, and the guys at Quiksilver edit it together with some action footage. I show the video at assemblies at a bunch of schools, then pass out stickers and posters so all the students will remember to buy Quiksilver gear.

Somehow, I promote the brand well enough to become a full-time employee for a couple years after the dot-com bust. In addition to my regular sticker-passer-outer duties, I organize the East Coast run for the Quiksilver Crossing. The Crossing is a seven-year surf exploration/marketing mission aboard the *MV Indies Trader,* the most famous vessel in surf history, as it previously led to the discovery of many Indonesian dream waves.

There are no new waves along the Atlantic for the voyage to uncover, only a string of raucous parties from

Miami to Maine. Afterwards, I have the job of editor for *Expeditions*, the magazine Quiksilver publishes alongside *Surfing* to commemorate each year of the journey. From gathering shots, to organizing the various sections, to assigning and editing stories, to writing the majority of the issue and finally seeing it in print, the process makes me wish I'd followed up on Hawk's offer to run *Surfer*.

During my time with Quiksilver, the company grows into a behemoth, but by 2005, they realize I'm useless at marketing, mainly because I can't stomach the whole "grassroots" narrative. All told, I spend twenty years with a Quiksilver sticker on my board (aside from the one year with Op). In that time, they give me racks full of clothes, foot the bill for me to ride countless waves, and pay me a decent amount of money. I'm thankful for everything I receive, especially considering how few surfers get anything at all.

The vast pool of recreational surfers hands their hard-earned bucks to their favorite companies, trusting that the logo on those trunks, or that wetsuit, will improve their ability to ride a wave or at least make them look cool. All the big surf brands are basically the same—similar overpriced apparel produced by cheap labor, offset by sponsorship dollars to prove they're as hardcore as they were when some guy first stitched the clothes in his garage.

I jump ship to Quiksilver's longtime rival Billabong, and coincidentally Quiksilver suffers a string of financial losses that culminates in a 2015 bankruptcy. The whole industry enters a period of major contraction, even before the coronavirus pandemic. Some of the companies revert back to being privately held, and Quiksilver actually purchases Billabong in 2018. Fewer people, it seems, are earning a living off surfing now than when I turned pro decades ago.

Does a booming surf industry make surfing better or worse? When business is great, all my friends (and I) get paid, not to mention the shareholders, VPs, designers, marketers, salespeople, customer-service reps, warehouse stockers and shippers, developing-world factory workers, skateboarding circus midgets, and bullshitting shop owners. And when business sucks, when the hype fades and the push to take the sport to a mainstream audience falters, we still paddle out and remember what makes surfing special. And it's not the money.

SEPTEMBER 2014

Rather than finding other activities to replace surfing, I find myself digging into the things I already enjoy, things I should've been doing more of all along. Now free from worrying about when the wind will switch offshore, I become a more attentive father. Without needing to care about whether the tide is rising or falling, I take more time to understand my students' needs. And in September, without feeling like I must obsessively track the path of each tropical system in the Atlantic as hurricane season reaches its apex, I find that getting lost in a writing session provides a similar satisfaction to losing myself in the ocean. And, as I rehash my loaded vault of surfing memories, I can't help but think about all the people who become old and decrepit without having ever experienced the thrill of walking on water. People like Gary Slaughter.

Back in 2004, Gary was my most regular surfing student. Regular, as in every week for four months. In truth, there was nothing regular about Gary. For starters, he was 72 years old, although he never divulged that information during our lessons. His dyed pewter hair made him appear younger, but he was hardly what you'd consider nimble. The most irregular thing about him was that after nearly twenty lessons, he still couldn't surf. In my fifteen years of instructing, with many thousands of success stories, Gary Slaughter was the first student I couldn't teach.

It should be understandable that, by late September of that year, I avoided his calls. Four months of shoving an old man into nosedives was enough for me, even if he was paying me sixty bucks an hour. His failure was my failure, and his phone number was a buzzing reminder of my ineptitude, one I didn't want to face. He may as well have hired a plane to write "Jason Borte Sucks at Teaching Surfing" across the sky.

The little I learned about Gary between pushes was that he'd grown up in New York but was a Red Sox fan, and his only other physical activity was cruising on his Harley. Neither of us was big on small talk, and he was usually too winded to speak anyway. Before our first lesson, on a muggy day back in June, he'd nearly keeled over from wedging himself into a full-suit in 90° heat, all before we'd paddled out. I made sure he signed every line on the liability waiver.

Gary's surf education wasn't a total loss. He could get most of the way to his feet, occasionally rising to a hunched, four-point stance consisting of two hands, one foot, and one knee. Then, he'd let go of the rails, and all hell inevitably broke loose. In bathtub-sized waves, his wipeouts were fantastic, as if he'd been blasted by an exploding underwater mine. His body contorted in a frenetic game of Twister, and he struggled in waist-deep water to extricate himself from the leash while gasping for the surface. He couldn't paddle by himself, but with me as his own personal pusher, he didn't need to.

I half-hoped he'd move on and forget about surfing, but perhaps inspired by his beloved Red Sox's inspirational charge toward the World Series that year, he kept calling. Gary promised to come clean about his age when (or rather if) he learned to surf, and I was curious. On the other hand, the days were getting shorter, and he was scheduled for knee surgery in November. It was now or never, or at least until the following summer.

Finally, I caved and called him back. Since none of my considerable array of camp boards had been stable enough for him, I dug deep into my storage unit and retrieved The Blue Whale, an old twelve-foot foam beast. It was a pain to haul to the beach, but if Gary was going to get up, he needed nothing short of a floating sidewalk.

For the first half-hour, the lesson was business as usual: watch Gary walk The Whale through the tiny wavelets to the lineup, wait for him to regain his breath, hold The Whale steady while he climbed aboard, turn the two of them around, choose an appropriate wave for him, give a heave, and watch in horror as he'd...crawl...up...almost... come on...you got it...yes...nooo!

I've fallen and I can't get up!

I clicked away the minutes until my, I mean Gary's, torture would end. He was so exhausted from his efforts that the muscles in his face lacked the energy to form any expression. But buoyed by some unknown call of duty, he trudged ahead. Meanwhile, I nearly threw out my shoulder hauling him into another gutless wave.

By this time, I couldn't bear to watch anymore. I scanned the boardwalk and spotted my friend Smitty on a mid-work surf check. Smitty was a project inspector for the city, but he seemed to spend more time inspecting the surf than inspecting building projects. I waved to him, but he didn't see me. *Ugh.* I checked my watch: only ten more minutes of agony.

Oh yeah, I'd sent Gary on another ride. When I turned back to view the carnage, there was none. No sign of The Blue Whale, and no epic struggle between the old man and the leash. Nothing.

But fifty feet further in, and a ways down the line, there he was. The Whale has a mind of its own: whatever way it feels like angling, you just go with it, a modern-day Nantucket Sleigh Ride. The board had decided to head north, and Gary had stood, let go of the rails, and managed to avoid detonating any mines. He was surfing.

An involuntary scream rose from my lungs. I splashed hysterically. Someone might've thought they were witnessing a shark attack. If a shark had tried to bite me at that moment, it would've choked on my goose bumps.

Gary, meanwhile, was afraid to move a muscle for fear of losing his balance. He rode along, as still as a hood ornament on a Cadillac. The Whale eventually dry-docked, yet Gary remained frozen a few more seconds before stumbling onto dry sand. He was done.

On the beach, I congratulated him, but he was too tired even to smile. He grabbed his towel and handed me his usual pre-written check, smeared with seawater. We agreed to meet again the next week, but winter barged in early with a big Nor'easter. Gary's knee surgery was approaching, and he didn't call. Swept up with my life, I didn't think of him again.

A few months later, I got a message from one of his friends: "Yeah, uh, I believe you are the surfing instructor for Gary Slaughter. I don't know if anyone has let you know, but Gary passed away. He said you had this little game going about how old he was. Well, he was 72." The friend explained that Gary was diagnosed with prostate cancer when he went in for his knee surgery, and he was gone a month after that. If Gary had any family, they were estranged. He prepaid to be cremated and wanted no funeral, not even an obituary. "I just wanted to let you know," the friend added at the end of the message, "that he really enjoyed surfing."

SURF SCHOOL

I'm hired to work as a camp counselor at Oasis Surf School, the first of its kind in Virginia Beach, in 1991. It's been nine years since I rode my first wave, but that span seems like an eternity. I've gone from a kid who'd only seen a handful of waves—and never one carrying a surfer—and who thought the fin on a board was supposed to face upward, like the dorsal fin of a shark, to a professional, now employed as an instructor. I'm surfing's version of the local golf or tennis pro, and I scarcely remember that clueless boy.

The first day of camp, maybe an hour into it, I witness magic. One of my kids slips off a few times while trying to get up, but is determined to get the hang of it. She's spent all of her eight years around the ocean, yet she hasn't stood atop a board and ridden a wave. After twenty minutes, she nails her stance and allows the eight-foot-long foam board to do the rest. When the energy peters out near the sand, she turns around, and the look on her face is priceless. She's now a different person, having performed the unthinkable. She's seen people do this but doubted she'd be able to accomplish the feat herself. She has walked on water. "This is the best day ever!" she squeals with delight.

Her look shoots me through time, transporting me back nine years to that same sense of wonder, and I feel it all over again. She rushes back for more while I spin another student around and send him off for the ride of his life. Yeah, I could get used to this. The pay is crap, and when I fall into my front door at the end of each day, I'm too exhausted to move. Regardless, the rewards are palpable. And working barefoot on the beach beats the hell out of dress shoes and a tie under fluorescent lights.

I work at Oasis for two summers before the camp folds. Meanwhile, as part of my promotional duties for Quiksilver, I accompany Matt Kechele to operate free, one-day camps up and down the East Coast. We pull into a different town each afternoon, swing by the local shops to corral their registrations, and show up at the beach the following morning to 100 smiling faces. Some of them already know how to surf. For many, it will be their first time. We get them hooked on riding waves, then load them up with enough Quiksilver freebies to ensure brand loyalty for life.

In 1997, as a new parent searching for additional revenue streams, I create The Surf School, my own little camp in Virginia Beach. There's no market analysis, no business plan—just me and a few foam boards. I throw together a paper flier and put it beside the register at WRV, the surf shop that sponsors me. Customers call for private lessons, and I organize a few summer sessions.

Each year, the camp grows bigger, and I eventually

establish satellite locations in North Carolina, New York, and Rhode Island. My business acumen remains as lacking as ever, and I still don't know a balance sheet from a bologna sandwich. Repeatedly, I mismanage my funds and remain clueless about ways to capitalize on potential growth.

The camp itself is a success. Every week, parents pull me aside to tell me what a wonderful program I have. Many have previously taken their kids to other area surf camps, and they're amazed at the differences. They say my instructors take such great care of the kids, and they come back year after year. Many campers enjoy it so much that, after several years as students, they come back as instructors. After twenty-plus years of business, I accrue all of three reviews on Google, never thinking to ask any of my repeat customers to share their experience for others to see.

Despite my continued failures as a businessman, my camps continue to earn a reputation for being a cut above the others in town. While I don't put much thought into my classroom teaching, I feel accountable for creating responsible surfers, people who not only respect other surfers, but are also future stewards of our beaches and oceans. And most importantly for parents entrusting me with their children, I make a point of hiring not the most talented surfers, but the most caring people. Conservatively, I estimate I'm responsible for at least 20,000 people riding waves.

Poll every surfer there is, and the consensus will be

that the worst thing about the sport today, the biggest threat to their happiness, is me. I'm the problem. Well, not me specifically, but crowds. There are more surfers now than at any time in history. And these hordes of new surfers, they'll say, are a result of the proliferation of surf schools. And I agree, sort of. I am the problem, and I'm here to say, "Don't send your kids to surf school."

I spent months of frustration and experienced countless spills before I rode my first unbroken wave at age 12. And, like the geezers who had to trudge miles to school, in the snow, uphill both ways, I'm a better person for it. The delayed gratification created a deeper appreciation for the act of riding waves. As the saying goes, nothing easy is worth doing.

When a "surf sherpa" drags your board down the beach, ferries you through the shorebreak, positions you in the lineup, chooses a wave for you, shoves you into it, and then barks an order when it's time to stand up, saying that you've then "surfed" can only be considered fake news. You've stood up, that's it. Most humans do that every morning of their lives. If you were placed beside the eighteenth hole at Augusta National on Sunday afternoon, only needing to sink a one-inch putt to win The Masters, would you feel like a fraud as your arms later slid into that green jacket?

So, I'm well aware of my part in the commodification of surfing. I am the problem. And if I'm the villain, the greatest evildoer of all time is none other than the most respected surfer in history, Duke Kahanamoku. This guy didn't just take folks surfing at his local beach (which he did for half a century); he circumnavigated the globe inviting entire continents to join the party. Yet somehow, no one is calling Duke a kook.

Surfing is cool. There's a countless stream of kids wanting to do it, and most of them have parents willing to shell out the money to make sure they learn in as controlled an environment as possible. Somebody is going to be tasked with the responsibility of teaching these children—and, to be honest, it should be me. Forget that some of these outfits are staffed with drunks, druggies, rapists, girlfriend-beaters, and thugs (and that's just the ones in my town); just as crucially, they're run by non-teachers. A good surfer does not make a good teacher. I mean, who would entrust their child to a week of Mike Tyson's Boxing Camp?

In 2010, under the guidance and prodding of my brother, I write a book, *The Kook's Guide to Surfing,* detailing everything I feel potential surfers need to know about riding waves. It's sort of a *Dummies* manual on the sport, with chapters on surfing basics, etiquette, equipment, waves, dangers, and tips for improvement. As a writer, former pro, camp operator, and licensed teacher, I'm uniquely qualified to bring surfing to the masses. I self-publish a few thousand copies and make runs to surf shops up and down the East Coast. The feedback is great, and I sell out within a couple months and place an order for more. I'm not proud of much and can't imagine being a salesman for anything, but this book is something I can get behind.

All my profits go into a reorder, and money is tight. Mrs. B is in nursing school, and I'm not bringing in what I did prior to the recession. I refinance our mortgage twice, each time skimming thousands off the top to knock down other debts. Then, I blow a fat equity line, default on one credit card, and max out another. With three kids (our third was born in 2008), two dogs, and a wife counting on me, I bungle our finances so royally that I run out of options. We are so broke, in fact, that I swallow whatever pride I have and return to the classroom as a substitute teacher.

After my first day of showing whatever video the teacher leaves for me to keep the students subdued, I get a call that promises to change everything. It's Perry Moore, a fellow Virginian who is living in New York. We grew up surfing along the same stretch of sand, but on different ends of town, so We've never met. His sister gave him a copy of my book for Christmas. He raves about *The Kook's Guide* and insists that it needs to be made into a movie. "That's what I do, by the way, take books and turn them into movies," Perry assures me. "You may have heard of them—they're called *Narnia*."

Perry was the executive producer for *The Chronicles of Narnia* series, among the highest-grossing film franchises ever. In addition, he's written a novel published by Disney's Hyperion label. His vision for *The Kook's Guide* is of a guy wanting to impress a girl, thus the guy reads the book and learns to surf. I haven't envisioned it as a movie, but within minutes I'm convinced. Perry promises a bidding war among publishers and a deal with Disney for the movie rights. The fact that I just resorted to substitute teaching in an effort to support my family makes this call all the more unbelievable, which, sadly, is what it turns out to be.

Two months later, I'm still substitute teaching, but that, I hope, is about to change for the better. I speak to Perry several times, and his vision is moving forward. I send him some copies of the book so he can "put them in the right hands" and am set to travel to New York for a meeting until a blizzard causes me to reschedule. I try my hand at crafting a screenplay and look forward to flying up to solidify our plan when I get some horrible news. There will be no trip, no bidding war, and no movie. Due to an unfortunate mix of prescribed medications for a back issue, Perry is dead. My status as a substitute teacher indeed changes—for the worse—as the job morphs into a full-time position.

OCTOBER 2014

Every autumn in Virginia Beach, we feel like real surfers. The flatness of summer has long since been forgotten, flooded out by recent memories of tropical cyclones, nor'easters, and various other wave-makers. We don't mind breaking out a thin wetsuit to offset the chill, knowing we'll soon be entombed in head-to-toe rubber. Our ears are clogged with saltwater from repeated dunkings, yet all seems right with the world. And, while we are far from eagerly anticipating the upcoming holiday season, we'll need it to repair any damage our multimonth surf-fest has caused to our jobs or our relationships.

2014 is no different, at least for those who answer the call. I watch flocks toting boards toward the sea to meet two legitimate swells that each last for several days. We vacate the tiny apartment below my parents' house, as Mrs. B has finished school and started working. We put our newfound income to immediate use by relocating to a spacious winter rental. Instead of being a whole block from the beach, we are now just a few houses from the sand. I find myself at the beach several times each day, walking the dog but paying far more attention to the ocean. By now, I appreciate every wave, no matter how sizable, shapely, powerful, or utterly lacking in all three attributes.

I'm still enjoying the reverie of mind-surfing, every wave ridden to perfection. Without being able to ride one for real, my mind inevitably searches for memories of my wave-riding past. I stare seaward and wonder if I have a single favorite. As I sift through my database in search of a superlative ride among a thirty-plus-year stream of them, nothing stands out. There are chunky Hatteras tube-rides, times I stood inside the barrel and felt I was orchestrating the entire ocean, and wild, throaty ones where my toenails barely clung to the deck of my board as I free-fell into the pit and beelined toward the safety of the shoulder. There are South African and Fijian freight trains, ruler-edged lines that seemed to be made in a factory. And there are Hawaiian bombs that lifted me out of my small-wave comfort zone, energy that had traveled unimpeded for thousands of miles across the Pacific before sensing the volcanic reef beneath it and lurching forward in a final, violent act. Strangely enough, all those epic rides mash together in my mind, none rising above the others.

The wave that stands out for me was barely a wave at all. It's the summer of 1989, and Virginia Beach is basically, typically flat. The crowd at 1st Street requires very little reason to show up, yet this afternoon there are no surfers, and for good reason. Solid southerly winds have kicked in, wrecking whatever semblance of swell is in the water, but not yet kicking up anything new. I won't paddle out on my normal board, because there's no way these sideways ripples could carry anything that small.

I'm bumming around the beach with my friend Chip, the guy whose parents would soon try to talk me out of becoming a teacher. We've been tight since back in the seventh grade when we nearly got into a fight during lunch for no other reason than we were both bored. Chip wears thick glasses and has a white spot in the back of his floppy brown hair from the skin condition vitiligo.

We swing by my then-girlfriend's house for a visit, but also because her dad has a shiny, new longboard in his garage. And, I remember, another old beat-up board as well. He surfed while in high school and is forever promising to "get back out there." Whenever I come around, he goes on and on about the days of the old steel pier that used to be at 1st Street.

Once my eyes acclimate inside his dusty garage, I dig through the mass of bikes and lawn equipment to reach the old board. I drag the thing into the light of day for a thorough inspection and see that it is wrong in so many ways. The outline resembles an Australian blobfish, a creature so void of form it was once voted the world's ugliest animal. Instead of pink, like the fish, the board's exterior is a faded, rotten brown. The rails on the board angle up rather than down, and it sports a scooped-out deck, a fat crescent tail, and a single skinny fin, all indicating it was some kind of drug-induced experiment gone wrong from around the time I was born. Chip happily grabs the new log, and I struggle to lift the brown blob, my arm too short to span its breadth.

The tide is dropping, so we paddle out to the sandbar at the end of the jetty. Tiny bumps emerge seemingly from inside the inlet rather than at sea, but they lack the propensity to break. Still, the girth of our boards allows us to muster enough paddling speed to stand and ride for a few seconds. Performance-wise, The Blob isn't suited for these conditions, or likely any conditions. Once moving, it seems to want no part of riding a wave, instead flopping around like a bratty kid who's been refused a packet of Skittles in line at the grocery store.

During any session, a wave comes through that is a little bigger than all the others, and it garners the title "wave of the day." We're only out there for about an hour, but this session's wave of the day is the one I remember. It can't be more than knee high as it rises sideways from the inlet. Luckily, I'm in the right spot and manage to coax The Blob into it. Truth be told, I would bully Chip out of the wave were he in position, as I'm kind of a jerk like that.

Usually, the fun of riding a big board is that it generates its own speed in weak surf, allowing the rider to flow with minimal effort. Not so with The Blob, as I have to widen my stance into a full squat to keep her from keeling over. I make it the distance of the day's previous rides and notice that this wave has another section that bends out to sea. Luckily, I stumble onto The Blob's sweet spot, so she doesn't put up too much of a fight. As I start to feel out her tendencies, we make it through that section and link up with another. The ride goes on like this for a while, angling out to meet up with an incoming peak, then slightly resetting our bearing toward the shore. There's no time to enjoy what's happening, as avoiding foundering requires my complete concentration.

The wave eventually peters out, and I exult in *Rocky*-like triumph, having vanquished my Apollo Creed—the petulant vessel beneath my feet. I look back toward the jetty, now far in the distance. Using the boardwalk hotels as a gauge, I see I've traveled two city blocks, which is unheard of around here. Somehow, I'm no closer to the beach than when I took off, having spent half the time riding out to sea. It's the longest wave I've ever ridden in Virginia Beach, and by far the weirdest. The fact that it comes on arguably the worst surfboard ever built only adds to the intrigue. I lug The Blob back to its spot in the garage, where it will live out its remaining days in anonymity. As far as I know, she never again sees the light of day, much less the ocean.

I've never made my own board, but I've been around enough shapers to see that they pour their heart and soul into every slab of foam that graces their racks. The process for these craftsmen is akin to birthing a child, each one the most beautiful thing their eyes have ever seen, the fruit of their loins, which they fill with love and knowledge and nervously send into the world and pray for its success. More than them garnering accomplishments, we want our offspring to be happy. Since a board has no emotions, all a shaper can ask is for a board to make someone else happy.

If only I knew who was responsible for The Blob, that godawful beast of a board. It would be a pleasure to let him know how I rescued her from dusty despair, if only temporarily, and how she's given me an unforgettable experience. As a shaper, hearing a story like that would make all the tediousness and the lousy pay and the inhaled chemicals almost worthwhile.

I never feel more like a surfer than after this wave. As much as I hate to talk about the act, or to be lumped in with other surfers as a member of some sort of tribe, I embrace the post-session endorphin rush. The camaraderie of sharing the experience with my friend makes the memory all the better. Our boredom led to adventure, creating a memory from a nothing day, as I challenged myself to best not some foe in a colored singlet but my own notions of what could be done.

I hear somewhere about how our memories are stored within the seasons, how certain weather evokes recollections that occurred under similar circumstances. If you move from your childhood hometown to a place with subtler weather changes, those memories get lost. I get that, but for me, it's not so much the weather as the waves. The sea has many moods, but eventually it begins repeating itself. At any moment, I catch sight of the ocean and am instantly reminded of a day, perhaps decades earlier, with similar conditions from my youth. Reliving my session with Chip and The Blob proves enough to get me through.

BAD TEACHER

A "real job" has never been a goal. Therefore, the only time I'm reminded of the countless hours I spent in classrooms learning about education are when I rifle through my office closet looking for some important paper and stumble upon my master's degree. *Oh, that's right, I'm an education major,* I think, and then toss the parchment aside and continue my search for some more important piece of paper. Otherwise, my degrees mean nothing.

I cruise through my 20s and 30s in a state of semi-retirement. I don't punch a clock, don't commute in traffic, don't have to subject myself to any daily, soul-crushing grind. Instead, as the years come at me, there's always a fallback gig to keep the dream alive. Pro surfing becomes writing, which becomes handing out stickers, which becomes showing people how to surf. Then, one day, Dan the mailman stops delivering checks, instead burying me in sternly worded letters from banks. I ignore these letters, of course, which seems effective for a while. But then there are three faces, each resembling mine, quizzical eyebrow and all, saying, "Dad, I'm hungry." For the first time, as I fall, there's nothing to catch me but that rolled-up parchment in the closet.

I look down, and my shirt is tucked in, and I'm wearing a belt and dress shoes. Where the hell did these come from? I look up, and thirty-five middle-schoolers stare at me from across their desks. This isn't how it's supposed to happen. I'm destined to do something great, not spend five days a week inside a mildewy room babysitting a bunch of ungrateful punks. Yet, that's where I am, and each of them expects me to lead them, to entertain them, to listen to them, to love them, and to hand them all the privileges I've been handed.

To add to the impossibility of the task at hand, most of my students lag way behind their peers. They come from broken homes. They are abused. They do drugs. They get pregnant. They have learning disabilities. They lack the basic amenities I grew up with. I don't know these kids. They subsist on 7-Eleven diets. They wear more expensive shoes than I've ever owned. They have as many ways of describing a fight as I do for waves. And each of them truly believes that, somehow, they'll miraculously become the next Kobe Bryant or Lil Wayne.

There's Isaac, a huge Samoan kid who shows up around once a month. He's a nice kid and completes his assignments on the rare days he's there. I meet with the guidance director to check off my year-end grades, and she sees that he hasn't come close to passing a single grading period. "Pass him," she says.

"But?"

"Just pass him!"

I have eighth-graders who suck their thumbs, a boy who pukes in his locker, a girl who eats all my chalk whenever I turn my back, and one who insists that the ghost of a small boy from the 1800s is standing beside us looking out my classroom window. I have kids with razor blades in their backpacks so they can cut themselves during the school day, or who have impaled a teacher with a pencil. I have a 17-year-old boy in eighth grade who already has a two-year-old daughter. I have a wonderful girl who gets As all year but gets baited into a fight in the spring, accidentally pushes a teacher who tries to break it up, gets expelled, and, from what I hear, is pregnant a few months later.

Regardless, my job is to prepare each of them for the be-all and end-all, the dreaded Standards of Learning (SOL) test. The mandate comes down from the state, to the district, to the principal, to the teachers, and to the students and their parents, and it is clear: this shit is serious. We sit through stern training with Jean, our Gestapo school-testing coordinator, during which we receive painstaking instructions on maintaining a sterile testing environment. Under the deceptive guise of a sweet Southern drawl and granny glasses, Jean details how any irregularities lead to audits and extra paperwork—and she despises audits and paperwork.

During my first year as a tester, one of my students tells me she's feeling sick. Earlier that week, a kid threw up in my trashcan, so I rush this girl to the clinic. She later returns to retrieve her belongings, saying she's going home. No problem: I exit her from the test and shut down her computer, proud of myself for having maintained a sterile testing environment. That afternoon, Frau Jean summons me to her office. "Close…the…door," she says with the chilliness of a serial killer, and she proceeds to ream me for violating the Third Reich rulebook. In my rush to avoid a complete and total barf-o-rama, I've forgotten that teachers are, under no circumstances, to touch a student's computer. I do my best to appear remorseful throughout the dressing-down, barely managing to control my laughter until I escape her office.

Years later, I get my students started on a writing SOL when a hand shoots up. It's Chuq (like "Chuck"), a pear-shaped kid who can't make the middle school basketball team but insists that the NBA is his future. The students are given a topical prompt for their essay. Chuq points at his screen and whispers, "I don't know what this means." Referring to slide 187 of our training PowerPoint, I recall that we can repeat the directions but are forbidden from reading the prompt, so I respond with the requisite, "Just do your best."

Chuq tries, but he isn't getting it. I have him reread the prompt: *Describe a time you saw someone commit a thoughtful act. And how does a thoughtful act benefit society?* He looks up at me and says, "I don't know what this means." He isn't stupid, but he can't make sense of the phrase. And he's no longer whispering. After I utter another patronizing "Just do your best," Chuq bursts from his seat. He's headed for the bookshelf, shouting, "Well, I need a dictionary then."

I can't allow him to reach the bookshelf, instead urging him to sit down and, again, do his best. How can he possibly write about something he doesn't comprehend? "What the fuck is a thoughtful act?" he yells. "I can't fail this fucking test!" The blitzkrieg of F-bombs clearly taints the sterility of the testing environment, so I shuffle Chuq out the door and wave down Jean. I've followed protocol, pretty much, yet my sphincter tenses as I imagine the "conversation" between them now occurring in her office. Moments later, Chuq struts through the door with a knowing smile. He hikes up his drooping jeans, sits at his computer, and starts typing. There will be no audit or additional paperwork, but the stench of irregularity is undeniable.

While I keep mostly to myself around school, teachers love to talk. For one employee's self-made rap video, he employs a few of his 13-year-old female students to shake their booties for him in the gym after school. One teacher, a religious woman, explains how she only had anal sex with her husband before their marriage, insisting it would've been sinful to partake in traditional sex. There are countless tales of extramarital affairs, many taking place inside the building and some during school hours. While I try to steer clear of all the classroom hanky-panky, I have a front-row seat when our two hottest female teachers grind all over each other one night at a bar.

Mixed with the weird and the tragic, there is also

plenty of frustration with the administration. When a student's behavior escalates beyond a detention or phone call home, the management could be expected to support the workers. More and more, taking the time to write a referral to admin becomes a lost cause. Either no punishment is given, or worse, the situation is flipped around to become an investigation of what the teacher did wrong. Given the amount of crap heaped daily upon a middle school teacher, it's no wonder I long to escape this predicament.

Fortunately, I have a few students in each bell who not only do what I ask, but also exceed all expectations. My influence on molding their beautiful, young minds is negligible, but they deserve credit for keeping me from losing mine. In classes of nearly forty children, at times I grow so irritated by my majority knucklehead population that I gather the "good kids" in a tiny circle for instruction and allow the untamed masses free reign throughout the rest of the room.

The model students are mostly girls, but they come in every color and background, proving that nurture trumps nature in creating successful little humans. Truth be told, every year there's a disproportionate number of Asians in the angelic posse. Whatever Tiger Mom feeds her young, it's working. An excellent follower of instructions is still a follower, but with an overcrowded classroom brimming with real challenges, I welcome any sort of reprieve.

From my experience, the current middle school model underserves our higher-achieving students. Our system changed from junior high to middle schools in the early 1990s, not long after I graduated. The thinking was that shifting the focus from subjects to students would facilitate a smoother transition for young adolescents. Sometimes, the system works, but it seems to me that endless coddling doesn't help prepare them for high school.

Not surprisingly, my biggest struggle is planning. Many teachers have multiple courses, and thus multiple lessons to create each day. I teach only one course, civics, so I'm only responsible for a single daily lesson plan. I inherit a year's worth of plans from my predecessor, and I repeat those lessons year after year. My kids' test scores are good, and I'm more consumed with maintaining order in my overcrowded classes than devising ways to challenge my higher-achieving students.

There is no way I am going to bring work home, but in school I do what I can to help the kids who need it most. I sometimes give them food or money, and in one class we raise $700 to help pay off delinquent lunch accounts. We have a student who is legally blind, and she does all her work using a tablet she brings from home. When I hear that her little brother has broken her tablet, I send an email requesting staff donations to replace it. In one day, we raise $300 and buy her a new one.

I make efforts to see my students compete in athletics, and I'm there to watch Ollie, a student who's done nothing but get pinned in his wrestling career, in his penultimate match. Add that he's been forced to repeat the seventh grade, kicked out of his beloved art program, saddled with a dorky pair of thick eyeglasses, and sports a face riddled with acne, and his years in this institution are an abject failure. On an evening when every other member of his team wins, Ollie is on his back by the end of the first period, staring up at the gym ceiling like he's done all season.

Thanks to the buzzer, Ollie escapes the near pin and seems buoyed by the small victory of pushing back the misery. Then, he not only staves off defeat but scores a few points to the delight of dozens of screaming fans from the retractable bleachers. And in the third and final period, Ollie shows *Rudy*-level determination against an unsympathetic opponent. Refusing to merely allow the clock to run out, he gambles his middle school life on flipping the script, Houdini-ing a reversal and pushing for a pin of his own. The whole gym stands and screams. The referee slaps the mat with fourteen seconds to go, and the place erupts. Ollie's superstar status lasts nearly a week, though, in his final match, he gets pinned.

The most wonderful student I have is a girl of Middle Eastern descent named Sevinc. She follows the rules, but she isn't content with what the state deems she should learn. Sevinc asks deep questions and seeks answers I cannot provide. I'm lucky enough to be her teacher for two years, as I move up from seventh to eighth grade at the same time she does. She's well-liked and confident but never conceited. Most memorably, at a time when anti-Muslim sentiment is at a fever pitch in America, she gives the class an impromptu explanation on the meaning of jihad. At the risk of being ostracized, she proudly describes how the term refers not to a holy war but an individual spiritual struggle against sin.

For years, I'm the inclusion teacher, meaning my classes mix run-of-the-mill kids with those in need of special services. Usually, the decibel level in my room is that of a house party. Then, my administration switches me to advanced classes. All of a sudden, I have entire classrooms of students who want to learn. Rather than doing everything in their power to avoid work, these kids turn in every assignment, usually before it's due. And if I neglect to check their homework at the beginning of class, they remind me. They blow through my trusty, old lesson plans, then bury their noses in novels. It's apparent that I'm not even close to being the smartest person in this room.

As a result of not having to spend most of my day worrying about classroom management, I grow bored and lazy. Okay, lazier. I no longer require new theatrics, don't need to mine pop-culture catchphrases to win my students' attention ("Ain't nobody got time fo dat!" "Cash me ousside, how bow dah?"). My little brainiacs take copious notes and call me out for any PowerPoint typos while I listen, with a strange envy, to other teachers' tales of classroom outbursts and rampant dysfunction.

It's difficult to fire a teacher, but a person can be moved to a situation that is so miserable it makes them quit. I dread getting moved from civics back to English, where I have to come up with new lessons and grade hundreds of student essays. Therefore, I do what I have to do to keep my administrator happy. I limit my surf escapes to when the waves are epic, and otherwise I show up to make certain nobody dies on my watch. It isn't a career, I keep telling myself; more like a gig to hold me over until something better comes along. I'm a stranger in a strange land, but there's always summer.

NOVEMBER 2014

When Earth was created, and all the species gathered for the evolutionary draft, humans must've been near the back of the line. Birds probably picked first. They looked at the size of this place and made the obvious decision, "With the first pick, birds select wings." And fish, I assume, were next, noticing the relative scarcity of land and announcing, "With the second pick, fish select gills." Somehow, the axolotl salamander slithered in at number three, snagging the Terminator-like ability to regenerate limbs and organs. With millions of species, when homo sapiens' turn came around, most of the really cool traits were off the board, so it was, "Geez, we'll take...um, cognition, I guess. What even is that?"

When I decided to take a year away from surfing, I wanted to see if it was possible and what would happen to me as a result, sort of like Morgan Spurlock ingesting nothing but McDonald's for a month. Self-reflection wasn't considered, but it was the inevitable result of removing the biggest constant from my existence. Apparently, when our rug gets pulled out from beneath us—the death of a loved one, a serious injury, job loss, no surfing—our response is to reflect. Our autopilot setting gets switched off, and cognition leads to introspection.

By November, I've dredged up a number of long-buried episodes from my life. Aside from offering smartass comments, I've never been one to share my thoughts, so people tend to come to their own conclusions about who I am. Through my blog, I find myself writing about incidents I've never discussed with anyone. Loved ones who've known me forever feel like they suddenly know me for real. More importantly, through this cathartic process, I'm beginning to get to know myself.

As much joy as surfing brings me, I was never comfortable with it being my identity. When I meet someone new, I often hear, "Oh, you must be the surfer." From the first time I got that line as a teenager, I cringed. "The surfer" to me was Jeff Spicoli, Sean Penn's "dude"-spewing stoner character from *Fast Times at Ridgemont High*. While I have the utmost respect for Penn and his performance, I'm embarrassed by the depiction. I know some guys who fit the Spicoli mold, but the majority of surfers I hang around with are nothing like that.

However, riding waves dictates nearly every choice I make in my life, so, like it or not, it's my identity. There was not a moment when I decided that surfing was my thing; I was just being a typical little brother, following in Derrick's footsteps, and suddenly this wave swept us up. After a while, Derrick mostly moved on to other pursuits, but he never stopped supporting all aspects of my career, from getting me sponsors, to showing up on the beach whenever possible, to wielding brutal honesty when necessary. I'm "the surfer," and he's known as "Jason's brother."

I'm having so much fun that I ride the thing for over thirty years. No one ever sits me down and says, "Hey, kid, there's more to life than surfing." Or if someone does, I can't hear them with my head buried in the sand. Surfing is my thing, but all this introspection begins to make me think maybe it isn't.

A year earlier, I took a trip with Derrick to Indonesia. He hadn't quit surfing completely. He got into television and film work after college and began directing commercials, and then later, feature films. He's been making films since 2009, and he spends the small amount of time he's home with his family. Each Christmas, he takes his wife and kids to Barbados, where he catches all his waves for the year. In 2013, he decides he wants to see firsthand why much of the surfing world has been raving about a group of Indonesian islands called the Mentawais. And since he hasn't surfed with his little brother in years, he coughs up enough airline miles so I can join him.

Traveling to Indonesia is a major undertaking, so fortunately my principal signs off on my extensive leave request. After a seven-hour drive, four flights, and a harrowing boat ride through heavy seas, we spend ten days surfing around the tiny island of Kandui. We just miss a major swell, but our stay is nevertheless filled with what I consider to be really good waves. We sample multiple world-class spots, all within a short boat ride, with little to no crowds. And, while we enjoy a nightly dinner of fresh fish and Bintang (the local beer), we're treated to photos of ourselves from the day's sessions on the big screen. I don't want to leave.

In all my travels, nothing rivals Kandui as a surf destination, even during an off week, but what's important about the trip is a story I hear from a fellow visitor. Directly behind the resort, there's a mellow spot called Four Bobs, and I venture out there on the slowest day of our stay just for something to do. Most of the guests are taking the opportunity to rest up, so the only guys in the water are an entertaining Aussie named Whitey and "Grub," his teenaged son.

Everything out of Whitey's politically incorrect mouth is a wisecrack. So, when he launches into another rant between waves, I hang off the side of my surfboard and eagerly await the punchline. Now 45 years old, Whitey worked construction until he noticed how much money was going to the lawyers who helped settle land disputes, so he earned his law degree several years back and cashed in. "I had to go to this professional-development-seminar bullshit last year," he begins, "and this bloke that was speaking laid it out for me."

Hmm, okay. Doesn't sound like the start of a funny story, but without a wave in sight, I feign interest. "So this bloke, he said to think of a circle with three rings inside it," Whitey says as he straddles his board, drawing a diagram in the air with his finger. His shock of white hair spikes outward in every direction, giving him a punkish air of Billy Idol mid-snarl. "In the outside ring you got your jobs, whatever random, meaningless jobs you've had, doesn't matter. On the middle ring, you got your careers. And on the inside..."

I ready myself for the payoff, invariably something outrageously homophobic, like all of Whitey's typically Australian musings. "...on the inside of the circle," his voice drops just above a whisper as if he's Steve Irwin approaching a mighty crocodile, "on the inside, that's your life's purpose, mate."

What the...is he serious? I didn't see a life lesson coming. "You find out what that is," Whitey deadpans, "and you're set." For once, he isn't messing around, and his story isn't finished. His voice returns to its normal level, and he adds, "So I went, 'Yeah, right. Fuck off, ya poofter.' And I never saw that guy again. Then a while later I was in India doing some work, and one of these Indian blokes says to me, 'You are like Shiva, the Hindu god of destruction.' And a light went off. I went, 'Shit, that's it. That's my purpose. I'm here to tear things down, break 'em into their parts, shit that's all fucked up and needs to be torn down. Then somebody else comes along and rebuilds it. That's my purpose.'"

The Great White One has spoken. I've known the guy for less than a week, but here he is, breaking character to lecture me on discovering my purpose. Is this his schtick? Is he really some sort of life coach masquerading as a foulmouthed surfer? Has Derrick arranged the whole trip for this moment, strategically dragging me 10,000 miles as an intervention? A small but inviting wave finally makes its way to the takeoff spot, so I spin and paddle. *Poor Whitey,* I think, *guy wasted decades before finding his calling. I found my life's work at age 12. Surfing is my raison d'etre. And I'm doing it.*

Now, after eleven months without riding a wave, I often flash on Kandui. When I miss surfing, I remember that, just a year earlier, I reached the ultimate surfing destination. Reflecting on the trip, my mind replays the dredging tubes over the shallow reef at Bank Vaults, the cold Bintangs on the boat rides back to Kandui, and the royal treatment Derrick and I received in our fully reclined business-class seats on the plane. But, inevitably, I come back to Whitey's story. The notion that surfing is my purpose strikes me, thanks to my hiatus, as the most selfish thought imaginable.

Plenty of guys have done it, devoted their entire lives to riding waves, most notably Miki Dora, one of the icons of the sport. After earning fame for his surfing prowess in the early days at Malibu and appearing in Hollywood surf films in the '60s, Dora took up residence in one country after another, utilizing various scams to support his lifestyle. His legacy, inspiring legions of surfers to give society the middle finger, suggests a life well-lived. But, as with Curren, there's only one Dora. My surfing might've inspired a handful of groms at 1st Street, but calling it my purpose in life is just plain stupid.

The amount of privilege I've enjoyed to this point embarrasses me. My life has been one gift after another, none of it—to my mind—earned. I can't see how anyone, not even Kelly Slater, who by then has returned to pro surfing and claimed eleven world titles, can suggest that surfing is his purpose in life. And if I refuse to grant Kelly that pass, there's no way I can use it myself. I didn't earn the trophies or the retainer checks or the exotic writing assignments. Surfing gave them to me, and I've patted myself on the back the entire time.

Like Whitey, I heard 'life's purpose' and went, *Yeah, right. Fuck off, ya poofter!* Now, landlocked and forced by my species' condition to overthink my situation, that's what I do. I cannot imagine a way that surfing this entire year, after more than thirty such years in a row, would have been a better use of my time than self-reflection.

At Socrates's trial for corrupting the youth of Athens with his questioning ways, he apparently uttered his famous maxim "The unexamined life is not worth living." I've heard a similar refrain throughout the year from fellow surfers regarding the "un-jazzed life" I'm choosing to live. Socrates was found guilty and sentenced to death—he, in fact, insisted he'd rather die than cease philosophizing. The best way to know a thing, I have found, is to get away from it. So, in the end, by downing poison hemlock in a forced suicide, Socrates got as far away from life as you can get.

Quitting surfing doesn't sound so stupid now, does it?

FAMILY

At 1st Street one day, I ran into an old acquaintance from back in Green Run. I hadn't known him well. All I remembered about him was that during a choral concert in elementary school, he was on the top row singing, and he fainted. He fell several rows to the stage, and then puked. When something like that happens in school, kids are way too jacked up to do any work, so it was the best day ever. Anyway, waiting for a wave at 1st Street, we got to talking about what we'd been up to since the faint-and-puke incident. I told him about my kids, and he asked, "Did ya marry her?" I responded, "Yeah, we were married for a few years before the kids came along." He gave me a weird look and said, "Wow, you did it backwards, huh?" Apparently, I'd broken protocol, at least according to how it's done in my old neighborhood. Either way, when I think about what I've done in life that I'm proud of, it isn't a good wave or a contest win or writing a book. It's my family.

Growing up, I don't give any thought to what I want as far as a family. I have a couple girlfriends in high school, but nothing serious. Just before twelfth grade, I meet Mrs. B. She's two years younger than me and as cute as can be. There is a mutual attraction, and the first time we hang out we play basketball at her best friend's house. She's such a genuinely nice person that my entire family loves her from the start. Pretty soon, we're inseparable, at least on land. The one time I try teaching her to surf, she drifts out beyond the waves to look at birds. From then on, when I surf, she plants herself on the beach.

Fast-forward five years. We move into a little apartment we call "the barracks" because of its blocky architecture and drab exterior. Considering We've already added a dog and a cat to the mix, we're basically a full-on family. I don't consider where the relationship is headed, but the soon-to-be Mrs. B drops not-so-subtle hints about getting married. I'm not opposed to the idea, but I don't care either way. One night as we're going to sleep, she chatters on about venues and guest lists, and I finally have had enough. I sit up and yell, "Why are we talking about this stuff when we aren't even engaged?" Then, on the spur of the moment, I add, "Well, do you want to?"

"Do I want to what?" she asks.

"Get married?" I say. She does, obviously, and with that, the lamest proposal in history is accepted.

Aside from making sure all my friends and family are invited, I leave the planning to her. I say, "Just tell me what time to be there." The countless details and hopes that everything will turn out perfectly make her nervous and stressed in the leadup to the wedding. My attitude the whole time is, "Whatever." Then, on May 7, 1994, we stand in front of 250 people, and the tables turn.

Looking gorgeous in a long white dress, Mrs. B is impossibly cool. She's made me promise not to turn up drunk, yet she's had a couple glasses of wine to calm her nerves. I haven't had a sip, and placed on the spot to recite my vows, I can hardly speak. The immensity of the situation is too much, and words refuse to come out. To keep from crying, I start giggling, and everyone bursts into laughter. Everyone, that is, except the pastor, who, from the stern look he gives me, is not amused. This is his church, and he seems to feel I'm making a mockery of his house of worship. He glares at me and says, "Let's get it together, son." I do, but barely.

We don't have a lot of money for a honeymoon, but we have plenty of time. It comes down to either enjoying a week somewhere in luxury or borrowing our neighbor's tiny "Wildcat" trailer and spending a month driving around the country. We pack the dogs in my pickup, latch the trailer on the back, and take off. My Toyota has a 4-cylinder engine, so making it up mountains with our added cargo proves a challenge. We trudge uphill at maybe 20 mph, and then fly down the backsides going 90.

"Driving around the country" really means hightailing it to California so I can go surfing. Other than pit stops at Graceland and the Grand Canyon, the remainder of the month is spent on the beach. I mail my entry fees for three contests before we reach the West Coast, so in effect I turn our honeymoon into a business trip. As with all the vacations we take as a couple, it's about surfing first and spending time together second. I even have a couple of my surfing buddies from home stay with us for a portion of the trip. Any time I'm in the water, I'm "working," so I don't consider it selfish. Besides, who doesn't love the beach? Mrs. B is a trooper, but three weeks into our surf honeymoon, she can no longer contain her frustration. We argue, and I take her to a theater to see the most popular movie of the summer, which, lucky for me, happens to be *Forrest Gump*. No one can be angry after watching that.

While we "did it backwards" by getting married years before having children, we get practice on the parenting front when we rent a spare bedroom to a young friend of mine. Zeke Sanders is a promising surfer who graduated from high school not long after I got married. We're renting my father-in-law's house near the beach, and Zeke desperately wants to be both "on his own" and closer to the surf. He's been diagnosed with bipolar disorder, and we do what we can to provide him with a stable home life. He's a little guy with a huge personality, unafraid to make bold fashion statements—including super-tight jeans and surgical masks years before anyone had ever heard of a virus called Covid—and call out any perceived injustices that he witnesses.

As an all-around boardrider (surf/skate/snow), Zeke possesses more skill than anyone in the area. My fondest memory of that time is driving with him to Ocean City, New Jersey, to compete in a weekend surfing event, the 1998 Heritage Pro. I'm 28, the reigning East Coast champion, and Zeke is an unknown 20-year-old punk. We stay in a friend's house who is out of town, so we have the whole place to ourselves. Zeke and I advance to the final day of competition, and we decide to prepare for our upcoming heats by playing poker and getting completely hammered, downing an entire bottle of liquor. The next morning, we not only show up on time; we're the last two left standing for the man-on-man final. The waves are small and weak, perfect for Zeke's tiny frame, and he wins the event. Afterwards, he says he feels bad for beating me, illustrating the disproportionate size of his heart.

One night in 2006, after drinking and arguing with his girlfriend, Zeke decides to take his own life. He made a half-hearted suicide attempt once while living with us, and we forced him to spend the night in our room so we could watch over him. He'd later moved into his own apartment a few blocks away, and we'd remained close but not close enough. The surfing community is rocked by Zeke's death, but for us it feels like We've lost a child. To honor his memory, I organize an annual contest for the local groms, Zeke's Lil' Rat Surfcus. To make it inclusive, we charge no entry fee beyond an optional donation to the local food bank. The event is just for kids and focused more on fun and games than on serious competition. Bringing smiles to so many children helps us all cope with the loss.

Other than prioritizing surfing, I see myself as a good husband. I have no work schedule, so I do my share of work around the house. My mom handled all the household chores when we were growing up, so the fact that I wash dishes and fold clothes makes me, in my mind, a saint. And when the kids come along, I cherish each moment of being a dad. I'm an early riser, so I make lunches every morning and walk my children to the bus stop. Then, I bullshit with my neighbor friends, go surfing, and do a little work before it's back to the bus stop.

Mrs. B doesn't go to college after high school but instead goes straight to work, first at a daycare facility, and then as a receptionist at a veterinary clinic. She stops working after our first two kids are born to be a full-time mom, which she is for around ten years. In her mid-30s, after her mom dies of ovarian cancer, Mrs. B decides it's time to follow her dream of becoming a nurse. Not only does she make it through school, but she thrives.

We get along well, but the mutual attraction erodes over time, as it does in most marriages. In its place, I harbor a growing resentment toward what she eats, how late she sleeps, and her lack of physical activity. Essentially, I become bitter that my wife's lifestyle choices show her blatant disregard for health and fitness. Every few years, she tries a new workout regimen but quickly abandons each one. She suggests we work out together, but the idea is ludicrous to me. I surf, so I don't need to work out.

I'm happy with everything else in my life, so I tolerate being in a marriage that is just okay. Not everything can be great, but since we aren't fighting, I figure we're better off than most. Besides, I can always go surfing. Even our closest friends and family assume we are perfectly happy. We met so young, and have been together for so long, it seems like a given that things will stay that way.

I'm not a risk-taker, and my family forms the safety net I can always count on.

Through it all, I remain faithful, at least physically speaking. I know people around town who cheat on their wives and seem to think nothing of it, which disgusts me. Mrs. B considers an emotional connection with another person just as bad as cheating. I disagree, mainly because if that's true, it means I'm unfaithful. Traveling as much as I do, it's inevitable that I meet people along the way, and there are times I get to know females in other towns. Once, Mrs. B discovers something I've written about a girl I met on the road, and we have serious conversations about splitting up. I assure her I'm committed to our marriage, so we decide to stay together. Sure enough, nine months later, my daughter arrives.

I devote myself to my family in the way I know how, by paying the bills, contributing around the house, and spending lots of time with my children. What I fail to do is work on improving our marriage. Mrs. B mentions counseling here and there, but I brush it aside. Just as our financial situation grows more unstable by the year, our relationship suffers as well. I don't know anything about managing money, and I'm clueless about navigating marital strife. In both cases, my response is to ignore the warning signs. What I do know, or what I've experienced throughout my life and assumed to be fact, is that whenever my situation seems bleak, there's no need to address the root of the problem. I just go surfing, and everything works itself out.

DECEMBER 2014

My son Grady is a bit of a philosopher. From the time he can speak, he asks insightful questions about how the world works and about life itself. He's not much of a student in the traditional sense, but he's a student of life. Whereas I spent a decade getting lectured in college classrooms, Grady has learned all sorts of things on his own and continually seeks the answers to life's mysteries. He's a high school senior, on his way to barely graduating and leaving school forever, as I near the end of my mission. A week into December, he sits beside me on the sofa one night and asks, "So, are you any wiser because of not surfing all year?"

The question almost seems condescending, like he's known all along it was a useless endeavor. This 17-year-old kid puts me on the spot and flashes his all-knowing, wobbly-headed smile that says, "See, I told you so." As much as Grady loves seeking answers and solving problems, he thinks that staying away from surfing amounts to a year flushed down the drain. "Am I any wiser?" I repeat, buying myself a few precious seconds as I struggle to drum up an answer he'll deem satisfactory. "That's a good question," I add, throwing in a few nods while grasping for something, anything, to prove to my child that his father isn't a complete idiot. All I'm able to conjure is, "I don't really know; it's not over yet." He's satisfied, alright—satisfied that he's made his point—and with that he gets up and leaves.

Only three weeks remain as I marinate on what wisdom has been revealed to me by abstaining from riding waves. I know I could survive a year, and maybe more, without surfing, and that it isn't my purpose in life, although I'm still unsure what my purpose is. I know that, although the water is now cold, and there are no waves on the horizon, I desperately want to surf, and to do so with my son. And I'm pretty sure that I'm not going to learn anything after fifty-two weeks that I haven't already learned in forty-nine. So, as Grady and his friends suit up on a gloomy Saturday afternoon to dive into the 50° Atlantic for a few waves, I join them.

I paddle out and sit up on my board. I'm encased in thick rubber from head to toe; nothing but my face is exposed, and that's all scrunched up from my ill-fitting hood. Any movement requires a concerted effort. I look around at a gray, flaccid ocean. Considering all the surf I've seen over the previous months, I can't have chosen a worse day for what feels like a monumental occasion. Grady and his friends chat away, not paying me any attention. To them, it's just another session on just another day in the blur that might later be remembered as the time of their lives. All in all, the day bears some resemblance to the one that birthed this idea over a year earlier.

A gray bump approaches, and I wonder if I'll be able to stand up. Only one way to find out. I wobble a bit but stand without falling. The thing isn't going to wait around all day for me to get my shit together; it's peeling away without me. I turn my attention down the line and set about generating speed to keep up. It has been decades since I've considered paddling, standing, turning, and pumping as separate elements—with repetition, the steps mesh into one seamless move, as with an experienced pilot orchestrating the various controls for takeoff. Despite my awkward deliberateness in transitioning between the stages of riding a wave, I do okay, at least until I try to go forward.

The most distinguishable aspect of my surfing has been my ability to go fast on sluggish waves. From my fastidious study of Curren, I long ago figured out how to harness each bit of energy to overcome uninspiring circumstances. It's a lot like swinging on a swing set, compacting and extending at the precise moments to go higher. That alone has separated me from most other surfers, especially considering the crap conditions on the East Coast. But, on this day, when I go to turn on the jets, the jets don't respond. In the next instant, my board submerges, and I plop forward into the cold water. No problem: It was my first try. Failure is to be expected.

I paddle back into position and wait with a little less patience. Another wave looms, and I make certain to be on it. Again, I get to my feet, angle down the line, press the accelerator, and hit what amounts to a patch of quicksand. Not since the winter of 1982 have I been physically unable to ride a wave, but that's now where I'm at. I didn't expect to pick up right where I left off in Puerto Rico a year earlier, but I hoped my skills might be on par with my surf-school students after their first three-day camp. My son doesn't say anything, but his face shows concern that his dad might've completely lost it.

Fortunately, I don't have to wait long for a third try. I take off on another waist-high peeler, sync with the rhythm of the ocean for a quick speed pump, and redirect my board into an arc off the top of the wave. In what turns out to be one fell swoop, my mojo is back. My son's worry changes into indignation that it only took me 10 minutes to climb back into form after a 333-day hiatus. Still, before long, he'll be packing up and relocating to California, so more than anything he's happy for us to be able to surf together.

My relationship with my children is nothing like what I experienced with my dad. He was a good parent, but he'd grown up at an early age. At the end of a long workday, he was tired. He wrestled around the house with me and Derrick and occasionally threw a football with us in the yard, but his involvement didn't go much beyond that. He hadn't lived my life of leisure, so working to support his family was the priority.

Becoming a dad is the best thing that ever happened to me. Surfing stunted my personal growth, so I still feel like a child myself. Working mostly from home while they were young, I can't get enough of being with them. From the time we bring each one home from the hospital, I love nothing more than taking them out for some impromptu journey. Whether on my bike, skateboard, surfboard, or on foot, we're usually on the go in search of adventure. It's my responsibility to see that we can afford whatever they need, but I don't let it get in the way of having fun. Seventeen years later, the "dad high" remains.

And that's what makes what happens next so difficult. Mrs. B finishes nursing school and begins working, so we're making enough money to move back into our old house. At some point that December, she mentions how she looked forward to the day that all the kids are grown and moved out so that it'll be just us. We can get a smaller place and travel whenever we want. For whatever reason, I haven't contemplated the empty-nest phase of our marriage. When she brings it up, the record that is my life screeches to a stop. *Wait a minute,* I think, *is that my future?* Even if we're planning on hitting up surf spots around the globe, I'm not sure I want any part of it.

There is no one I respect more than Mrs. B. She is as caring and giving of a person as anyone I know. Together, we've survived decades of ups and downs. Most importantly, we've created three amazing little people, each of whom I love more than anything else in the world. But in our marriage, the love seeped out years ago. I realize that a relationship requires work, but both of us have neglected our duties for ages. I know that it's normal for couples to experience rough patches, but this feels like something bigger. We don't argue, but we also don't show affection toward one another. We're more like roommates than spouses. As parents, we aren't setting a good example of what a healthy relationship looks like.

When we met, we were children ourselves. When we got married, we were still kids, neither of us having a clue of who we wanted to become. We "did it backwards," as my old schoolmate said, yet we defied the odds and persevered. A year without surfing has taught me that operating on autopilot is no way to go through life. Mrs. B can't be what I want, and I can't be what she wants. For someone so full of love, there is no way she could truly be happy with what We've become. Neither can I. And for the first time ever, just before the year ends, I tell her so.

SHIVA COMES FOR MY LIFE

Looking back on my year in drydock, I can't fathom my life without having done it. A surfing hiatus is not something I ever wish to repeat, but its value for me at the time is immense. All in all, stepping away might be the best decision I ever made. That December, when my son asked if I'd become any wiser as a result of staying out of the water, I had no answer for him, and it's easy to see why. At that time, I was still living without the biggest constant in my life, in amidst the most radical upheaval I'd ever experienced. I was an old house stripped to the studs, knowing a rebuild was coming but with no blueprint for what it would look like.

How much of a role, if any, Whitey's tale about finding purpose plays in my decision to undertake this adventure is questionable. His Four Bob's spiel doesn't cross my mind when I decide to begin the project, or at any time throughout the process. I've pretty much forgotten about it. Until I lay my story out in words, delving into the timeline of my life years later, I never consider that it might have played a part. One way or another, I went to Indonesia and met Whitey, and the next year I quit surfing, setting lots of other changes into motion.

I'm still a surfer, so on the surface that hasn't changed. When I get the urge, I do it, regardless of the conditions. As my most memorable ride on The Blob suggests, a board exists for every set of circumstances. "There are no bad waves," as the legendary surfer Mickey Munoz once said, "only a poor choice of equipment and a lousy attitude." I derive equal enjoyment from gliding across unbroken ripples on my eleven-foot surf/paddler as carving turns on my shortboard. My goal, more than ever, is channeling a wave's energy, honoring the final phase of its life with my dance.

As much as possible, I try to remove all vestiges of competition from my mind when I'm in the water. Old habits die hard, and every so often I see someone surfing well and, without thinking, I'm mentally right back in a contest jersey and channeling everything into outdoing that guy. Luckily, it doesn't happen often. I see OMG Wes competing in the Old Fart division in the local amateur events, and I want no part of it. Instead, I make a point to strike up conversations with strangers, looking for every opportunity to improve someone's day.

According to my mom, when I was a toddler, my favorite saying was, "You're not the boss of me." Whenever someone told me to do something, that's how I'd respond. Then, surfing became the boss of me. Now, I enjoy riding waves more than ever, but it no longer controls me. Coming back from my yearlong break, I pay little attention to forecasts, which are usually wrong anyway. Thinking there's going to be surf leads to unneeded stress. If a friend calls and tells me there are waves, I'll go surfing. That is, if my schedule allows it. If I don't have the time, I don't go—and I'm fine with it. My relationship with the sport is in a much better place.

Meanwhile, Mrs. B and I agree to consider counseling around the time I get back in the water, but it never happens. I remain intent on making our marriage work, and the following summer we move back into our house. There are some minor repairs to tend to from our renters, and I set about fixing what I can. When I'm re-staining the porch on a steamy August day, a feeling of dread stops me in my tracks. I look at the porch, and the house, which we'd designed together so long ago, which my father had built, in which we'd raised our kids, and in which we plan to grow old. The notion comes into focus that our marriage is a lost cause, like I'm out here straightening deck chairs on the Titanic. I reconsider the idea of counseling, but I know it will only delay the inevitable. The sooner I leave, the sooner we can each find happiness.

Living without my kids, even every other week, scares the hell out of me. Nothing is as important to me as my children. If there's one thing Mrs. B and I do well, it's making fantastic little humans. I consider whether staying together is good for their development, and ultimately, I decide that having them see a relationship devoid of mutual respect isn't helping anyone. I tell Mrs. B I'm finished on a Sunday morning, and two days later we gather the kids and share the news. They take it all in stride, as best we can tell, and within a couple weeks I move out.

My first night without my children happens to be the night before I have to show up back at school after summer break. The weight of my decision hits all at once, and I drink to numb the pain. I lean on old friends to get me through as I adjust to my new normal. Sunday is kid-swap day, a strange ritual that is rife with emotion. As young people do, ours adjust without much difficulty.

I've dropped a bomb on Mrs. B, so it takes some time for her to get beyond the initial hurt. As soon as I leave, I feel completely different toward her. All the years of built-up resentment immediately vanish. I have nothing but respect for her as a mother and as a person. Over the next few months, we manage to work out an amicable divorce agreement free of loathsome lawyers, and I hope she considers me as good a friend as I do her. As I tell anyone who asks about her well-being, she's the best ex-wife ever.

In 2016, I'm inducted into the East Coast Surfing Hall of Fame at a ceremony during a trade show in Orlando. Years earlier, I attended one of these ceremonies to introduce OMG Wes for his induction. I utilized what Steve Hawk had taught me, "Seek first to entertain, then to inform," sharing all sorts of embarrassing stories about Wes. Afterwards, I would've felt bad, except I was just following the example I'd learned at 1st Street from Wes himself.

When I'm inducted, my parents, Grady, and several friends from home are there to support me. The room is packed with legends from the sport, guys I grew up admiring in magazines. I've spent months writing and rewriting my speech, but I'm still so nervous that I'm twitching. I speak about how lucky I've been to grow up with the family, the friends, and the opportunities I had, but any accomplishments that got me here mean nothing to me. I long ago tossed out all my trophies, and probably wouldn't have attended the ceremony had my parents not already purchased their flights to Florida. I say that it's what I do with my position, how I give back, that matters. I think about what surfing can do for kids who wouldn't otherwise get that opportunity. Overcoming their fears and riding a wave shows them that they can do anything, and giving them that chance, purely as a confidence-booster to follow their own path, has become my mission. By the end, I'm overcome with emotion and barely keep from bursting into tears.

Since my middle school students don't take me up on the offers to teach them how to surf, I work with the school system to create a free program for underprivileged kids. The folks downtown provide us with a school bus, and we take groups from several local schools for a day at the beach. I continue with the event every year, servicing mostly students from the middle school at the beach, the one where I worked back in 1999. Our kids predominantly come from two trailer parks near the oceanfront, and for nearly all of them it's their first experience with surfing. Despite their living so close to the beach, the chance to learn to ride waves would otherwise not be available to them.

Driving through my old Green Run neighborhood today, I wonder what my life would've been like had my dad not started making money and moved us to the other end of town. There's only so much to do here that doesn't involve some sort of trouble. Without finding that door to my real-life Narnia, I likely would have taken a vastly different route. I was given the world, and my goal is to provide the same opportunity to as many other people as possible.

In the classroom, I soldier on, feeling in some way that teaching is slowly repaying a debt for the life of privilege I've been given. At least I have my summers. After a few more years in middle school purgatory, I get a call from an out-of-the-box principal who's been referred to me by a mutual friend. The principal has an idea for a new high school elective, sort of a makerspace, and he believes that my varied background makes me the ideal candidate to teach it. I'm offered more-or-less free reign regarding the curriculum, but I'll need to come in during the summer to get everything ready for that upcoming fall.

I've never so much as checked my school email over the ten previous summers, so I have to give the matter some serious thought. After a good five minutes of letting all these factors settle in, I accept the position. How can I not?

Here's a course in which each student will undertake a project of his or her choosing, and my job is to provide guidance along the way. We bring in some area business owners I know and ask them what qualities are lacking in young job applicants. Each time, we get the same answers: that graduates need to get better at communicating and solving problems. Using my contacts around town, I help each student secure a consultant who is a professional in that student's chosen field. From there, each kid applies the principles of inquiry to create a project. There's no textbook, no quizzes, and no Standards of Learning test.

Unlike before, I believe wholeheartedly in what I'm selling. This course is, hopefully, the future of education, and through continued tweaks it continues to improve. The school provides the tools, and the students set out to create video games, movies, books, blogs, podcasts, photography exhibits, go-karts, doghouses, fundraisers, clubs, or any invention they can dream up. All I ask is that they submit a proposal, build and maintain a website to track their progress, and create a TED Talk explaining what They've learned at the end. I feel the class goes a long way in preparing these kids for life, and I look forward to every day I go to work. When I pass other teachers in the hall, they ask me how it's going, and my response is, "Livin' the dream!" They laugh, thinking I'm kidding. Believe it or not, I now look forward to the end of summer break, as I can't wait to meet a new batch of students and hear what they want to create.

I can't help but reflect on my fateful session with Whitey, back when I was certain that surfing was my purpose in life. I see now that my purpose is helping others find their version of surfing, the individual path that will take them to places beyond their imaginations. Riding waves did that for me, and now I get to cultivate these kids' interests in hopes of igniting a spark. The course teaches me that the best students aren't the rule-followers, the ones who've been trained to do whatever a teacher asks of them. No, the ones who thrive in my class are the individuals who question authority, question convention, and question the system. They may have found nothing but failure in our outdated educational structure, but here they can succeed so long as they try.

After decades of only taking a trip if it revolved around surfing, I learn to appreciate the food, scenery, and culture found in waveless locales. Of course, if I happen to be somewhere and find out there's a wave, I'm going to ride it. On a family trip to Montreal, I look online at area attractions and come across video clips of a standing wave in the Saint Lawrence River. I carve out an hour one afternoon to make my way to the river, and sure enough, several people are enjoying the endless, waist-high left. I reach into my pocket and offer the first guy I see $20 to borrow his board. He laughs at me, but the next dude bites. On my first try, I don't paddle hard enough, and I miss the wave, leading to a shameful twenty-minute paddle back to shore. Luckily, he gives me one more shot, as well as some pointers. I catch the wave, do thirty or so turns in the next two minutes, and leave completely satiated, my thighs burning from the strain.

The reason I'm in Canada is a woman named Feeling Chery. I scoff at dating apps until, bored during a few faculty meetings, I help a coworker decide whether to swipe left or right. After about a year of living single, I dip my foot in the water on an app called Plenty of Fish. I see it as the only way to meet someone outside my bubble, and, sure enough, a few weeks into it, I meet Feeling. Her parents are Haitian, but they immigrated to Montreal in the 1970s. I'm smitten from the moment we meet at a restaurant in VB, and a few months later, we're dating.

Feeling and I make a great team, and she makes me a better person. With her influence, I'm more thoughtful, organized, healthy, and happy. She's gradually trying to teach me to dance, and I'm attempting to make her into a surfer. So far, neither of us is having much success. We date for a few years, get married in 2020, and I look forward to every moment of growing old with her.

In answer to my son's question, I don't believe that my year without surfing filled me with wisdom. I still do stupid things every day, and I don't foresee that ever changing. What the year provided me was perspective, and that's something I wouldn't have gotten had I continued coasting in default mode. Again, I'm not any wiser for having taken that year, yet I believe it was wholly worthwhile. Any wisdom was in listening when the idea first bubbled into my consciousness. As ridiculous as it sounds, my body knew something my head didn't.

Sigmund Freud wrote extensively about a moment in each of our lives when we finally understand ourselves, a point at which we see that everything is connected. I consider the events of my life to be unrelated until I sit down and throw them all into one giant pot. When I stir it up, it becomes obvious that seemingly disparate areas are all intertwined. Strangely enough, Freud referred to the sensation as "oceanic feeling." For me, I needed to escape the ocean to find it.

ACKNOWLEDGEMENTS

This book was a product of the pandemic. If not for the world shutting down in 2020, and all my students refusing to log into Zoom meetings, I would not have found the time to do this.

None of this would exist without Brad Melekian. His 2013 article "Surf No More, Forever," from The Surfer's Journal, planted the seed for this project.

Thank you to Sequoia Schmidt (such a badass!) for thinking my story was worth sharing. And to the entire team at DAP Books, including Alma Felix and Shelli Sherwitz for keeping everything in line, Matt Samet for his editing, and Kim James for her design.

To Mo Sanford and Andrew Tonra for providing photos for the cover. Also for their friendship and support throughout my journey.

To my brother Derrick for leading me to water, for having high expectations of me in anything I do, and for demonstrating how to accomplish goals.

To Ken Hunt for decades of guidance, support, and friendship. Also for fighting against this experiment the entire way, forcing me to reevaluate my position and ensure that the endeavor was worthwhile.

To Smitty for being a wonderful friend, surf mate, story teller, and sounding board for my often hairbrained ideas.

To Steve Avery and Jesse Fernandez for introducing me to books.

To Steve Hawk for helping to build a clueless wannabe writer into a slightly less clueless one.

To my parents for allowing us, and urging us, to be who we are, and for supporting my pursuits whether they agreed with them or not.

To my children for trusting me with my most important and favorite job ever. This was written so they could better understand the irresponsible kid who they turned into a father.

To my wife Feezy for supporting this and all my endeavors and for helping me see the world through a clearer lens.

ABOUT THE AUTHOR

Jason Borte is an educator, entrepreneur and author of the recent Virginia Is for Surfers. A former professional surfer, he is a pro champion, longtime camp operator and East Coast Surfing Hall of Fame inductee. His books include Pipe Dreams: A Surfer's Journey and The Kook's Guide to Surfing. He lives in Virginia Beach with one eye permanently fixed on the ocean.

ABOUT THE PUBLISHER

Di Angelo Publications was founded in 2008 by Sequoia Schmidt—at the age of seventeen. The modernized publishing firm's creative headquarters is in Los Angeles, California, with its distribution center located in Twin Falls, Idaho. In 2020, Di Angelo Publications made a conscious decision to move all printing and production for domestic distribution of its books to the United States. The firm is comprised of eleven imprints, and the featured imprint, Catharsis, was inspired by Schmidt's love of extreme sports, travel, and adventure stories.

www.ingramcontent.com/pod-product-compliance
Lightning Source LLC
LaVergne TN
LVHW091053080826
845145LV00002B/727

* 9 7 8 1 9 6 2 6 0 3 4 7 8 *